# PASTORAL PRAYERS FOR THE HOSPITAL VISIT

### Edited by

### Sara Webb Phillips

Abingdon Press
*Nashville*

### JUST IN TIME!
### PASTORAL PRAYERS FOR THE HOSPITAL VISIT

*Copyright © 2006 by Abingdon Press*

All rights reserved.

*This book is printed on acid-free paper.*

#### Library of Congress Cataloging-in-Publication Data

Pastoral prayers for the hospital visit / edited by Sara Webb Phillips.
    p. cm. — (Just in time!)
    Includes bibliographical references and index.
    ISBN 0-687-49658-6 (binding: pbk., adhesive : alk. paper)
    1. Church work with the sick—Handbooks, manuals, etc. 2. Sick—Prayer-books and devo-
tions—English. I. Phillips, Sara Webb. II. Just in time! (Nashville, Tenn.)
    BV4335.P3765 2006
    2648.13—dc22

                                   2005029128
ISBN 13: 978-0-687-49658-7

09 10 11 12 13 14 15—10 9 8 7 6 5 4

MANUFACTURED IN THE UNITED STATES OF AMERICA

# CONTENTS

# ACKNOWLEDGMENTS

When approached about writing a collection of hospital prayers for pastoral use, I realized that, no matter what the situation, my prayers would all sound very much alike. I suspect that is true for many clergy; we have our own prayer language and poetic style. From that realization, I decided to solicit prayers for various situations from a range of experienced pastors. I am grateful to Kathy Armistead at The United Methodist Publishing House for recognizing the value in this approach.

These prayers come from a variety of sources—pastors, laity, bishops, chaplains, seminary professors, and students—representative of several ecumenical traditions. Although edited for consistency, these prayers come from the heart and experience of persons who are practiced in praying with others. I wish to express my deep gratitude to those who contributed prayers and comments to this book: Rev. Mark Adams, Bishop Edsel Ammons, Rev. Dr. E. Byron Anderson, Rev. Elizabeth Andrews, Rev. Jenny Arneson, Rev. Dr. Dori Grinenko Baker, Dr. Nancy Bedford, Rev. Tommy Blackwell, Chaplain Nancy Braund Boruch, Rev. Edgar Brady, Rev. Dr. Jack Bremer, Rev. Dr. Gennifer Benjamin Brooks, Dr. Lisa Burkhart, Rev. Jaylynn Byassee, Ms. Judith Campbell, Bishop Kenneth Carder, Rev. Jane Cheema, Rev. Michael Coffey, Mr. Ted and Ms. Jennifer Collins, Rev. Robert and Ms. Becky Crocker, Mr. Max Davis, Dr. Jane Doyle, Chaplain Betsy Eaves, Mr. Lionel Edes, Rev. Dr. John Fairless, Rev. Linda Farmer-Lewis, Rev. Dean Francis, Chaplain Kate Mezzenga Guistolise, Rev. Dr. David Handley, Rev. Mark Horst, Rev. Mary Hubbard, Rev. Sara Isbell, Ms. Eileen Mezzenga Javurek, Ms. Carolyn Keith, Rev. Yul Kwon, Rev. Dr. Steve Lobacz, Ms. Christine Martin, Rev. Lee

McKinzie, Mr. Jeff Moore, Rev. Young-Mee Park, Rev. Dr. Ed Phillips, Rev. Kathy Barba Pierce, Rev. Dr. Marti Scott, Ms. Barbara Mason Skinner, Rev. Dr. James L. Travis, Rev. Rebecca Grinager Trefz, Rev. John Wagner, Rev. Dr. Greg Waldrop, Rev. Gaston Warner, and Ms. Letechia Williams. Time to edit this volume came through the generosity of my Evanston congregation and The Louisville Institute's Sabbatical Grant for Pastoral Leaders.

I am always thankful for my partner in life and ministry, Edward Phillips, and my community of friends and family, who not only contributed to this volume but have prayed with and for me through much of my journey. I am indebted to those who taught me to pray: my parents, grandparents, wonderful Sunday School teachers and seminary professors during my formative years, and colleagues in ministry. And, of course, I have learned much from the people of the congregations and communities with whom I have prayed as pastor, colleague, and chaplain over the years: Kenton; Tennessee Extended Ministry; the First United Methodist Churches of South Bend, Indiana and Evanston, Illinois; Broadway Christian Parish of South Bend; Trumpet Call Community; and the campus communities of Lambuth University in Jackson, Tennessee, the University of Notre Dame, and Union College of Kentucky.

With the Apostle Paul, I can truly say "I do not cease to give thanks for you as I remember you in my prayers. I pray that the God of our Lord Jesus Christ, the Father of glory, may give you a spirit of wisdom and revelation as you come to know him, so that, with the eyes of your heart enlightened, you may know what is the hope to which he has called you, what are the riches of his glorious inheritance among the saints, and what is the immeasurable greatness of his power for us who believe, according to the working of his great power" (Ephesians 1:16-19).

Sara Webb Phillips
Pentecost 2005

# INTRODUCTION

As a seasoned pastor, I make my living with words through preaching, teaching, praying, and written reflections. I have been called upon to pray at a moment's notice in a wide variety of settings. With such experience, one might think I would never be at a loss for words. Yet there have been times when my emotions have overwhelmed me or joy has made me speechless; at those times I have fumbled through prayers. I have held the hand of parishioners as they died, mourned with families immediately after the death of a loved one, rejoiced at the bedside as doctors relayed good news, and held the brokenhearted in my arms as they learned of tragic news. Although God's grace is always at work in our lack, I have sometimes wished that I could have been more composed in bringing an appropriate word in the midst of difficult situations.

I also bring the patient's perspective; a tragic accident, several surgeries, and time at the bedside of my critically ill child have deepened my understanding of suffering. I know firsthand the experience of struggling with pain, being out of control, hoping against hope, and praising, doubting, being angry, and pleading with God. The prayers that were offered for me and for my family during these times brought much comfort in the middle of chaos, and returned my thoughts to the One who formed me and loves me through this journey of human life.

This small volume of hospital prayers is an effort to place into a pastor's or lay visitor's hands a resource for praying in a variety of situations for which one may not be sure of how or what to pray. It also can serve as a catalyst for more varied prayer and for ways to offer comfort at the bedside. This book provides models to help patients offer their own prayers. There are suggestions for singing together as well.

Although this volume is designed to be carried into the hospital and its table of contents offers easy reference to prayers for particular situations, I suggest that you spend some time going through the prayers, either devotionally or in focused preparation. All of us in pastoral leadership will be called upon unexpectedly at times. Unless one is a chaplain in the hospital with resources readily at hand, having already reflected on these models will aid us in our ability to be present and focused upon the person and families in need. I also commend to your reading the wealth of prayer books and denominational worship resources that include prayers for the sick and dying.

A few notes about these prayers. First, prayers of this nature are always particular—for a unique person in a unique situation. They are not printed here in the abstract "O God, I pray for *(Name's)* healing in *(his/her)* pain," which can be awkward to read, but rather use a name and the appropriate pronouns. Just be careful, should you use these prayers directly at the bedside, to insert the correct name! Of course, the more personally you can speak to situations from your knowledge of them, the more meaningful your prayer may be to them. Including persons in the room at the time of the prayer (family members, friends, caregivers) would also be appropriate.

Second, I have offered a variety of names for God. Most of them are interchangeable with any prayer. Not only does this remind us of the innumerable ways to express who God is, but may provide an image of the Holy One that gives added strength to the patient. I also often ask patients how they address God, and then use their own prayer language to add familiarity and comfort.

Third, Scripture passages are included as a way to preface the prayer. Selections are taken from the New Revised Standard Version, with Psalm 23 also listed in the King James Version because of its poetry and familiarity for many older persons. I have maintained the integrity of the translation but want pastors to know that I am sensitive to the numerous male pronouns and images for God. I have tried to select passages that minimize these references; I tend to rephrase the reading for particular situations (i.e., a woman raped by her father may need to hear a different term for God than "Father" at that moment of distress). Our awareness of the need to grapple with this sensitivity is, in itself, a healing of the wounds in the church. Remember though, that the hospital bedside is not a time to make a theological point. Knowing parishioners will help guide the language of prayer.

Four, these prayers reflect a sense of hope for healing, while at the same time realistically addressing the serious nature of many of the situations. Healing can come in many forms, and our prayers should always reflect God's ability to work in a variety of ways. Sometimes, when I was certain patients would not live through the night, not only did they survive, they actually recovered enough to go home. "What god is so great as our God? You are the God who works wonders" (Psalm 77:13b-14a).

Over the years I have gained some pastoral wisdom through the privilege of being with persons through their hospital experience. Some of the basic learnings are:

## When to Visit

The best times to visit patients are late morning before lunch, early afternoon right after lunch, and late afternoon. Tests, therapies, and procedures are usually completed or not yet begun around those times. Early morning visits do not allow time for the patient to have bathed and could be awkward or embarrassing for them. Sometimes my schedule has not permitted a visit until later in the evening. For many patients, that is a lonely time of the day when activity has slowed down, family has left, and it is too early for the later dose of pain medication or sleeping pill. Some deeply spiritual conversations have been exchanged in those quiet moments.

## Access to Critical Care Patients

Intensive Care patients have very limited visit times but hospital staff often make exceptions for clergy who stop by briefly to pray. Wearing a clergy collar or a hospital name badge (most hospitals provide them for local clergy) can provide more access as well.

### How Long to Visit

Brief visits are always in order. Remember that the patient is there for treatment and/or recovery, even when it is a happy circumstance.

### Where to Sit

Never sit on the bed when the patient is in it, even if invited to do so. Not only is it unprofessional, a slight shift of position may be painful for the patient.

### Patient Requests

Use good judgment if a patient asks you for assistance. Offering candy that is out of reach or providing an arm to get out of bed may be counter to recommendations of doctors or nurses. You can always offer to get hospital staff for the person's aid.

### Flowers

Although altar flowers are often given to persons in the hospital, always make sure your patient can tolerate the particular variety. Carnations are almost always safe; roses and other fragrant flowers can trigger allergies. (The strong scent of lilies can be nauseating or even make one think of a funeral parlor!) The person may also enjoy a bulletin of the service from which the flowers came.

### Respect Privacy

Respect the need for privacy, should doctors or therapists be conversing with the patient when you enter the room. Often, however, particularly for older persons, the patient and medical personnel are pleased to have another pair of ears to hear and help explain to the patient, and perhaps to family later on, what is being discussed.

### Out-of-town Family

If you become aware that an out-of-town family member is going to visit, you may wish to try to be at the hospital to meet them. This not only lets them know the church is responding to the needs of their loved one, but also establishes a relationship, should there be critical needs in the future.

### Leave a Card or Note

Always leave a business card or a note indicating that you have stopped by. For those patients who cannot communicate or who might forget your visit, a brief note—about the time you visited or what the person mentioned to you—is helpful for family members. On a few occasions, I was the last visitor with whom a patient communicated before death. It was a comfort for loved ones to know their family member shared prayer before loss of consciousness or death.

### Uncommunicative Patients

Remember that persons who appear uncommunicative can often hear, so be careful of words and tone of voice around the patient. Encouraging persons to squeeze a hand or blink as a response to questions, or to offer "Amen" to a prayer, enables two-way communication. I have been with persons who have not spoken for days, who, during prayer, have begun to mouth the Lord's Prayer with me, or sing out on a familiar hymn.

### The Power of Touch

There is much comfort in human touch. With increased cultural sensitivity about entering another's personal space, I recommend that one ask permission before taking a hand, or laying a hand on a shoulder or brow. Not only does it respect the patient's body, it offers them a degree of control in an environment where sometimes little choice remains, and also highlights the intentionality of personal connection. If given permission, I hold the hand of a patient for prayer, and also invite family members to do so around the bedside. I may also lay a hand on the brow of a person confined to bed, as a parting touch. Be careful that the patient is not in an awkward position with IVs, or has to strain to hold a hand or turn a head in order to see you.

### Rituals and Worship Practices

Do not overlook the rituals and worship practices of the church. Many churches are reclaiming the rites of anointing and recognizing the value of more frequent participation in the sacrament of Holy Communion. I encourage you to purchase a vial of oil (available at many Christian bookstores and herbal shops) and to obtain a traveling Communion kit. These sacred actions carry a power all their own. Brief rituals for anointing with oil and offering Communion at the bedside are included in chapter 6.

In the same way, reading Scripture can help express the wide range of human emotions. An appropriate Scripture passage begins each selection; additional suggestions are included in chapter 4.

I frequently offer to sing a favorite hymn. The lyrics of some hymns, appropriate to share in a variety of situations, can be found in chapter 3.

I almost always end a prayer by leading into the Lord's Prayer. Several prayers in this book reflect this approach.

### In the Name of Christ

Finally, prayer is what we offer because we come in the name of Christ, as representatives of Christ's body the church. Sometimes it may seem awkward to offer a prayer with a doctor there, or as attendants come to get a surgery patient. Most often, I find that the patient is appreciative of prayer at these moments, and that hospital personnel are usually pleased to join in the circle of prayer or are willing to wait respectfully. The few times I have been embarrassed or rushed, and left without offering a prayer, I have felt I let the person down and missed extending the church's ministry to them. Providing prayers of grace and peace is, of course, our basic purpose for visiting patients; we are ambassadors from the congregation on behalf of no one less than Jesus Christ himself.

It is my prayer that this book will be useful to you as you seek to serve God's people who experience time in a hospital. Whether they move toward physical and emotional healing or their healing comes in the world beyond this one, may you be a faithful conduit of God's healing love and grace. As Ephesians 6:18 says, "Pray in the Spirit at all times in every prayer and supplication. To that end keep alert and always persevere in supplication for all the saints." May it be so with all who serve God through hospital prayer ministry.

# PASTORAL PRAYERS FOR HOSPITALIZED PATIENTS

## RELATED TO ILLNESS OR SURGERY

### 1. Facing Surgery

**Scripture**

The LORD is my shepherd, I shall not want. / He makes me lie down in green pastures; he leads me beside still waters; / he restores my soul. He leads me in right paths for his name's sake. / Even though I walk through the darkest valley, I fear no evil; for you are with me; your rod and your staff—they comfort me. / You prepare a table before me in the presence of my enemies; you anoint my head with oil; my cup overflows. / Surely goodness and mercy shall follow me all the days of my life, and I shall dwell in the house of the LORD my whole life long. (Psalm 23)

**Prayer**

Gracious God, we come this morning asking that you continue to bring your comforting presence to Ann and all who care for her. As she faces surgery this morning, we ask that you calm any fears and anxieties she may be experiencing. Bring to her a sense of your ever-present spirit and of your hope, that she might experience wholeness and fullness of life.

Carefully guide the surgeon's hands, eyes, ears, and heart that your healing touch might be felt through the doctor's skill. Be also with the surgical team and the hospital staff that will care for Ann in the days ahead that they might be instruments of your mercy.

Sustain her husband, Robert, and her children, Stacie and Connie, and all who love and care for her, that they may trust in the presence of your steadfast love and be upheld by the prayers of our congregation.

Bring your Holy Spirit upon Ann and embrace her in a circle of hope, courage, and community. Bind us one to another that together we may live toward fullness of life. All this we ask in the name of Jesus, the great healer of us all, who taught us to pray: "Our Father who art in heaven..." Amen.

# 2. After Successful Surgery

### Scripture

> You who live in the shelter of the Most High, who abide in the shadow of the Almighty, / will say to the LORD, "My refuge and my fortress; my God, in whom I trust." / For he will deliver you from the snare of the fowler and from the deadly pestilence; / he will cover you with his pinions, and under his wings you will find refuge. (Psalm 91:1-4a)

### Prayer

God of glory and might, we thank you for your healing power at work within Charles's body. We are grateful for the skill of the surgeon and all who assisted to bring this child of yours through surgery. We are relieved that the prognosis looks good, and that he will soon be active again.

We pray now for good rest, for quality care from the hospital staff, and the loving attention of Charles's family in the coming days of recovery. For all the blessings you give us, we praise you.

For all the trials we experience, we ask your grace and mercy. For it is in Jesus' name we pray. Amen.

# 3. After Surgery That Was Not Successful

## Scripture

> One thing I asked of the LORD, that will I seek after: to live in the house of the LORD all the days of my life . . . / For he will hide me in his shelter in the day of trouble; [God] will conceal me under the cover of his tent; he will set me high on a rock. / Now my head is lifted up above my enemies all around me . . . / Hear, O LORD, when I cry aloud, be gracious to me and answer me! / Do not hide your face from me. (Psalm 27:4-7, 9a)

## Prayer

Almighty and Loving God, we thank you for all the blessings with which you have graced us this day—for love of family and friends, beauty found in the world, the comfort of home, times of productive work, and for the gift of life itself. I lift up Henry in this moment. We are grateful for the doctors and nurses who have tended him and brought him through this surgery. We are anxious about the outcome, and trust that your presence will guide him as he walks this lonesome valley. Do not hide your face from him, but keep him near, granting healing and strength in the coming days. Ground Henry's faith deep in your house forever, for we pray as Jesus taught us: Our Father . . .

# 4. Anticipating Bad News

## Scripture

> We have not ceased praying for you and asking that you may be filled with the knowledge of God's will in all spiritual wisdom and understanding, so that you may lead lives worthy of the Lord . . . May you be made strong with all the strength that comes from his glorious power, and may you be prepared to

3

endure everything with patience, while joyfully giving thanks to the Father, who has enabled you to share in the inheritance of the saints in the light. (Colossians 1:9b-10a, 11-12)

### Prayer

Cleansing and Renewing God, we come before you this day filled with so many emotions—fear, uncertainty, and frustration—as well as faith and hope. We know the way in which you have walked beside us through the many ups and downs in our lives and yet we call upon your presence now more than ever. We want to know what the future holds for us, yet the fear of what that might be threatens to consume us. Calm that fear, Lord. Wrap your loving arms around Rebecca and help her feel your peace and confidence to face the unknown, to realize that you are always with us.

Gracious God, just as Jesus asked if it be possible that this cup would pass from him, there is part of us that wants to ask the same; that we not have to face the news we may hear and what that will mean for our lives. But Lord, we ask now that you give us the courage that Christ had, in order to also pray, "not what we want but what you want, O God." Help us know that what you want is for us to walk in relationship with you through both the good and the bad that life may bring. All this we ask in the name of our Savior, Jesus Christ. Amen.

## 5. Diagnosed with a Serious, Progressive Illness

### Scripture

O God, you are my God, I seek you, my soul thirsts for you; my flesh faints for you, as in a dry and weary land where there is no water. / Because your steadfast love is better than life, my lips will praise you. / So I will bless you as long as I live. (Psalm 63:1, 3-4a)

**Prayer**

God of creation, all of life is your handiwork. You have known and loved us, your children, since before our birth. At this time of great anxiety over what this illness means for Carolyn's future, there is one thing we know for sure; that you will continue to be with her throughout her life journey. Reassure Carolyn and give her strength and courage for the special challenges ahead. Strengthen her relationships with family, friends, and church community that she and they might find comfort in one another and in you. We especially ask your blessing upon the medical team caring for her. We ask all this, knowing that you know our every need even before we ask; through Jesus Christ our Lord. Amen.

# 6. Recovering from Heart Surgery

**Scripture**

> Create in me a clean heart, O God, and put a new and right spirit within me. / Do not cast me away from your presence, and do not take your holy spirit from me. / Restore to me the joy of your salvation, and sustain in me a willing spirit. (Psalm 51:10-12)

**Prayer**

Our most gracious God, today you are continuing what you have begun through the hands of so many people—Lee's recovery. Help him do the things that make it possible for him to get better. We know you as a God who has given us embodied hearts to sustain physical life and spiritual hearts to open us to heavenly life. May Lee's heart continue to pump life-giving blood so that he may infuse life-giving hope and purpose to the world in which we live and to the people whose lives he is privileged to touch.

We thank you for the healing already begun through the skill of doctors and nurses, and the miracle of this surgery. Now give Lee strength to do his part in rehabilitation to get stronger.

Support his family, who walk this journey with him. In the name of our individual healer and the healer of all nations, Jesus our Lord. Amen.

# 7. Suffering from a Stroke

### *Scripture*

> Where can I go from your spirit? Or where can I flee from your presence? / If I ascend to heaven, you are there; if I make my bed in Sheol, you are there. / If I say, "Surely the darkness shall cover me, and the light around me become night," / even the darkness is not dark to you; the night is as bright as the day, for darkness is as light to you. (Psalm 139:7-8, 11-12)

### *Prayer*

Dear God, our help in times of trouble, we know that Max has lost the sense of who he is. He has achieved so much: work accomplishments, worldly success, intelligence, and his independence. But now it is a struggle simply to talk and walk. Please show him that his identity is not measured by what he achieves. Help him understand his purpose in life and follow the path that you have prepared for him.

Show us that, through your love, we have the strength to follow our life's path through mountains and valleys, because you are at our side to guide us. Especially let Max know of your presence in a powerful way through these next days of rehabilitation. Help him understand that he has always been dependent on your care and love. Now help him accept the support of others. Give Beth and their boys the strength and patience to help in ways they never contemplated.

Give Max the courage to work hard at recovery but also to accept what he may not recover. Let him not cling to his old life, but give him the faith that you will show him how to live a new and different life.

Help him find gratitude in his life and show him ways to contribute to the well-being of others, not only his friends and family, but those less fortunate. Show him how to continue to be the giver and not just the receiver of love, concern, care, and support. Show Max ways to laugh again and hope again. Like Jesus' passion on the cross, our darkness is followed by light—the light of new life, the light of lasting peace. We pray in that name of peace—Jesus. Amen.

# 8. Dealing with Cancer

## Scripture

> "Therefore do not worry, saying, 'What will we eat?' or 'What will we drink?' or 'What will we wear?' For it is the Gentiles who strive for all these things; and indeed your heavenly Father knows that you need all these things. But strive first for the kingdom of God and his righteousness, and all these things will be given to you as well.
>
> "So do not worry about tomorrow, for tomorrow will bring worries of its own. Today's trouble is enough for today." (Matthew 6:31-34)

## Prayer

Life-giving Creator, you formed our inward being and knit us together in our mother's womb. Now your child Jenny needs your strength and presence in her life to face the hours and days of living with cancer. Remind us again, God, that you are always at work to bring good in the midst of all things; even the pain of our weakening bodies caused by the invasion of illness. When we find that all we can do is cry out to you and desperately plead for relief from pain and sorrow, hear our prayer, O God, and strengthen our resolve.

Healing God, renew Jenny in your love this day and grant her hope and life as a gift of your faithfulness. Grant her the strength to face each hour of this day and every day with courage and gratitude, and help her not to worry. May she know the signs of your healing and sustaining presence that are ever about us. Surround her with your comfort to ease the suffering and uncertainty of this cancer. Especially grant strength and comfort to her family, as they undergird her with love. May all of us learn to greet each day with prayerful thanksgiving. But when we cannot pray as we ought, because our pain and sorrow is too overwhelming, let the interceding of your Spirit be a presence beyond any words that can be spoken.

God, we thank you for the life we know in this day and we commit our lives into your loving care. We offer you now the faith we have and ask that you strengthen it and sustain Jenny in this time. We pray in the name of Jesus the Christ. Amen.

# 9. Coping with Breast Cancer

### Scripture

> Give ear to my words, O LORD; give heed to my sighing. / Listen to the sound of my cry, my King and my God, for to you I pray. / Let all who take refuge in you rejoice, let them ever sing for joy. Spread your protection over them, so that those who love your name may exult in you. (Psalm 5:1-2, 11)

### Prayer

Loving God, unto whom all hearts are open, all desires known, and from whom no secrets are hid; we come in prayer today, because you have come to us by your Holy Spirit moving us to seek you. A diagnosis of breast cancer is fearsome for Eileen on several levels and we do not know where to start our prayers. Medically, breast cancer has invaded her body, turning her world upside down. There are so many new treatments, so many decisions to make about which path to take. This kaleidoscope of options and overwhelming information breeds anxiety about making the wrong decision. So many folks try to be helpful by sharing their stories. Help Eileen know her experience is its own unique journey, and that she doesn't have to meet the expectations of those survivors who paths seem less challenging.

Psychologically, Eileen feels attacked at the very core of her being as a woman. She fears surgery, a possible carving away of her body. She doesn't want to lose her hair, no matter how many "adorable" wigs and turbans are offered. What will this mean to her future relationships—will she ever feel whole or safe again? How will she balance caring for herself, her family, and work? How will she respond with grace to well-meaning friends who need more care than they give?

There are financial pressures as well. Even with insurance, treatment is costly, and it is tiring to order medicines and keep up with the paperwork. But you, O Lord, are the God of strength and love. We know that even when you feel so very far away, you *are* present. Help Eileen to turn her worries over to you. Give her courage to face this illness, and peace that only you can bring. Be with her healthcare team, granting them wisdom and power. Enable her to see more clearly the really important things in life—love for you and the relationships with family and friends, and trust in your everlasting presence. Be with her in the dark stillness of the night and the crazy bustle of the day. Let her rest in your loving arms, knowing that you will do far more than she can ask or imagine. For we pray in Jesus' name. Amen.

# 10. Undergoing Chemotherapy

### Scripture

> Look on my misery and rescue me, for I do not forget your law. / Plead my cause and redeem me; give me life according to your promise. / Salvation is far from the wicked, for they do not seek your statutes. / Great is your mercy, O LORD; give me life according to your justice. (Psalm 119:153-156)

### Prayer

O God of the downtrodden and the lonely, we thank you for the gift of life that we know is so precious at times like these. We pray your blessings upon Barbara as she finds herself in need of health and healing once again. We had hoped that the first round of chemo would have been enough to defeat this disease.

We pray for the staff that administers this treatment. Help Barbara trust those who prescribe for and treat her. We thank you for their patience, kindness, and eagerness to lend help and offer hope.

Give Barbara peace after this additional treatment. Grant her family peace and acceptance that, whatever may come, she is secure in God's love for her. She has lived fully, and given so much to so many. Accept our gratitude for the many blessings with which you have surrounded her. In these next days of soul tiredness, debilitation, and just feeling lousy, grant her the comfort of the Spirit's companionship and the promise of life everlasting. For we ask it in the name of the Prince of Peace whom we serve. Amen.

# 11. Suffering from Addiction

### *Scripture*

> I waited patiently for the LORD; he inclined to me and heard my cry. / He drew me up from the desolate pit, out of the miry bog, and set my feet upon a rock, making my steps secure. / He put a new song in my mouth, a song of praise to our God. / Happy are those who make the LORD their trust, who do not turn to the proud, to those who go astray after false gods. / Be pleased, O LORD, to deliver me; O LORD, make haste to help me. (Psalm 40:1-3a, 4, 13)

### *Prayer for One in Rehabilitation*

Renewing and Refreshing God, you are the source of all healing and wholeness for all those who suffer in mind, body, and spirit. Through your power and grace, help Harold turn to you and let go of his fears and face the road to recovery with honesty and courage. Be with all of those affected by this disease, especially in this place of healing and recovery, and grant them hope and faith as they reach out to support one another toward the possibility of new life. In the pain of these next days, let Harold know you are healing him. Enable his family to have patience and forgiveness toward him, and strength to move through this time, day by day. For we pray through Jesus Christ our Lord. Amen.

### Prayer for One Not Yet Confronting Addiction

Dear Lord of All Feelings, you have known us every day of our lives; you knew us before we were even born. I pray for Hudson, who is loved by you, perhaps even more than he loves himself. Grant him to know and feel your love this day. I pray that Hudson may understand that, even in his powerlessness to control his own life, you, O God, are powerful and always present. Please be strength for him when he is weak. Give Hudson just what he needs for this day; teach him to live one day at a time. In the name of the One who suffers when we suffer, yet always gives us hope for peace within our souls, Jesus our Lord, we pray. Amen.

## 12. Unable to Diagnose the Source of Illness

### Scripture

"Ask, and it will be given you; search, and you will find; knock, and the door will be opened for you. For everyone who asks receives, and everyone who searches finds, and for everyone who knocks, the door will be opened. Is there anyone among you who, if your child asks for bread, will give a stone? Or if the child asks for a fish, will give a snake? If you then, who are evil, know how to give good gifts to your children, how much more will your Father in heaven give good things to those who ask him!" (Matthew 7:7-11)

### Prayer

Faithful God, here and now, we confess to immense frustration. So much is lost with Mary's illness; so much is unclear. We are sometimes hopeful, often fearful, and always wondering what is happening, and what is going to happen. We seek answers but also ask for strength and patience to live in the uncertainty of waiting.

We pray for those in the medical community who are seeking a solution. We ask blessings for their perseverance, their patience, and their wisdom. We ask your blessing for Mary and her husband Andrew. Help me as their pastor to know how to give comfort in this confusing and alarming situation. And yet, O Lord, most of all we ask for your peace, your perspective. Allow us, especially now, to put our full trust in you. We ask this in the name of Christ. Amen.

# 13. In Need of a Transplant, Waiting for an Organ

### Scripture

> How long, O LORD? Will you forget me forever? How long will you hide your face from me? / How long must I bear pain in my soul, and have sorrow in my heart all day long? / Consider and answer me, O LORD my God! / But I trusted in your steadfast love; my heart shall rejoice in your salvation. (Psalm 13:1-2a, 3a, 5)

### Prayer

God of Word and Promise, we come to you waiting. We try to wait patiently but we are not always successful. Steve needs a chance for a new life through a kidney transplant. In your Son, Jesus Christ, there is life, and it is in his name that we ask that you be with Steve and his family as they await an opportunity for a new physical life. Renew his spiritual life as well, opening him to your grace and new beginnings.

We ask that you grant Steve patience, comfort, and strength as he waits to hear from the doctors. In response to this potential gift, we pray also for the life that must die in order to share life. We give you thanks for that life and the promise held for that person, and remember the family and the trauma they will experience. Lord, be with all of us as we wait—calm us, love us, and keep us in the palm of your hands. We pray this in the name of the One who is Life, Jesus Christ. Amen.

# 14. In Chronic Pain

### Scripture

> Then I saw a new heaven and a new earth... And I heard a loud voice from the throne saying,

"See, the home of God is among mortals. He will dwell with them as their God; they will be his peoples, and God himself will be with them; / he will wipe every tear from their eyes. Death will be no more; mourning and crying and pain will be no more, for the first things have passed away."

And the one who was seated on the throne said, "See, I am making all things new." (Revelation 21:1a, 3-5a)

### Prayer

God of Fire and Whirlwind and the Still Small Voice, it is one thing to hurt and another thing to hurt all the time. It is one thing to walk through the wilderness and another thing to live there for forty years. For my brother, Mark, I ask that in this troubled place you would be a comforter; that in this dry place you would be a cool fountain; that in this desert place you would be a blooming flower. Come by here, sweet Jesus, and touch us with your hand of blessing. Quench the fire of suffering; gird him with the armor needed to battle this difficult foe of pain.

God, it is one thing to pray and another thing to pray without ceasing. Take this pain and hear it cry to you. We ask this in the name of Jesus, who knew our suffering and pain, and triumphed over it into new life in which we share. Amen.

# RELATED TO CHILDREN AND YOUTH

## 1. Celebrating the Birth of a Child

### Scripture

People were bringing even infants to [Jesus] that he might touch them; and when the disciples saw it, they sternly ordered them not to do it. But Jesus called for them and said, "Let the little children come to me, and do not stop them; for it is to such as these that the kingdom of God belongs. Truly I tell you, whoever does not receive the kingdom of God as a little child will never enter it." (Luke 18:15-17)

## Prayer

God of life and love, we praise you this day for your wonderful work in the birth of this child Elizabeth. For the safe pregnancy, successful delivery, and now for the miraculous presence of this beautiful daughter, we give you thanks. We pray for Sara's continued recovery, and strength for the important role of mothering this new life; and for Andy, that his love as a father will reflect your own.

How marvelous are your works, O God! How amazing the tiny fingers, toes, ears and eyes, the inside and the outside of baby Elizabeth whom you have brought to birth! How wonderful your plan for us, that we are placed into families to surround us with your love. You embraced children and offered them as a model that we all might live in joyful and innocent ways. We pray your blessing upon this baby and her parents, Sara and Andy, that they might continue in joy and peace and gratitude each and every day. In Jesus' name we ask it. Amen.

# 2. Mourning a Miscarriage

## Scripture

A voice is heard in Ramah, lamentation and bitter weeping. Rachel is weeping for her children; she refuses to be comforted for her children, because they are no more. (Jeremiah 31:15)

## Prayer

O Lord, our Hope and our Redeemer, be present with us in this moment of loss. The expectation of new life that Jeff and Kathryn held in their hearts is now broken, their hope shaken. Despair threatens them. Bring them your strength, O Lord. Lift them up and hold them with your mighty and merciful hand. Remind us that this child—this special life formed by you—rests in your arms, surrounded by your heavenly angels. What we had hoped for is now gone. What we had dreamed would be has vanished before our eyes.

Gentle God, in the depth of such pain and desolation, embrace Kathryn and Jeff and their families with your compassionate love. Be still with them when words cannot come. You know pain deeper than our soul can express; yet somehow, in your own mysterious way, you give us hope through your glorious Son. As Rachel wept, so we weep for this child whom we knew in our hearts and treasured while in this mother's womb. Show us your holy love beyond all understanding. We pray all these things in your holy name. Amen.

## 3. Grieving the Loss of a Baby Near Birth

### Scripture

> O LORD, you have searched me and known me. You know when I sit down and when I rise up; you discern my thoughts from far away. / Where can I go from your spirit? Or where can I flee from your presence? / If I say, "Surely the darkness shall cover me, and the light around me become night," / even the darkness is not dark to you; the night is as bright as the day, for darkness is as light to you. (Psalm 139:1-2, 7, 11-12)

*The following prayer has been written specifically for the woman who has given birth and then lost the baby, or given birth to a stillborn child. This grief is particular and unique because of the baby's physical closeness to the mother during the months of pregnancy. If the child's father, siblings, or other family members are present, the prayer should be adapted to include their loss as well.*

*Whenever possible, speak the name of the child who has died, if one has been given. In prayers, church bulletins, All Saints Day services, and follow-up conversation, it is often extremely comforting to family members to hear their child's name spoken. Speaking the child's name in this prayer helps the mourners establish the reality of their grief from* the immediacy of the hospital room to the days, weeks, months, and years to follow.

### Prayer

Gracious and Loving God, may your spirit enfold and embrace Sue, filling her with your love in this place. Encircle Sue and her family in these moments of loss and suffering too deep for words. The waters of the womb held life that is no more. Sue's arms long to hold this beloved child, Sophia; her body aches to nurture her baby. Our tears seem to have no end. Our minds strain to understand what went wrong. We feel a huge emptiness where we had expected such joy. Gracious God, help Sue survive what seems unsurvivable. Help her body, her mind, and her spirit be open to the love and care of others. Help her to yield to the soothing presence of your Holy Spirit as you feel her pain and know her anguish.

In the days ahead, we pray that Sue may find holy listeners, people who will help her find ways to express her sadness. May she find times of solace, when the clouds of grief seem to open and she remembers who she was before this tragedy. May she find quiet, soulful moments when she is able to begin piecing back together the fragments of her being. May Sue's family and friends find ways to pause in the rush of life and be present to Sue in her grief, and to acknowledge their own loss.

May Sue receive the treasure of a deep connection to the spirit of this beloved child, Sophia, who spent too brief a life within her body. As these days of grief turn to weeks and months, we pray for healing of her body, torn and bleeding; healing of her mind, doubtful and confused; healing of her spirit, bruised and deflated. May the memories of pregnancy—special movements, hiccups, times of quiet wonder—return to provide Sue with comfort when she is able to receive them. May she be reminded, in the moments when she feels alone, that grief is a wave that must move through her in its own time and its own way. In the coming days, may she know the healing power of God's love through the church family and through the great cloud of witnesses who have departed and now embrace this beloved child in your eternal presence. We ask all these things in the name of Jesus. Amen.

# 4. Mother Choosing Adoption for Her Newborn

### Scripture

> Yet it was you who took me from the womb; you kept me safe
> on my mother's breast. / On you I was cast from my birth, and
> since my mother bore me you have been my God. / Do not be
> far from me, for trouble is near and there is no one to help / my
> heart is like wax; it is melted within my breast; / my tongue
> sticks to my jaws; / But you, O LORD, do not be far away! O my
> help, come quickly to my aid! (Psalm 22:9-11, 14b-15b, 19)

### Prayer

Dear God of Strength, because Meredith loves this child, she
chooses for him a life of hope, to grow up in a family where he
will be cherished and nurtured beyond what she is able to give at
this time. Her heart aches, for this is the hardest thing she has
ever done. O Lord, she needs your strength.

Be with this child, watch over him, and protect him every day
of his life. May he always know that his birth mother loves him
greatly. Grant to the parents who receive him a depth of love and
care that will embrace Meredith as well.

Grant her your healing strength as her body recovers after delivery, and your abundant grace as her spirit heals from this wise, but
difficult decision. Grant her peace; in Jesus' name. Amen.

# 5. Adoptive Parents Receiving Their Child

### Scripture

> How lovely is your dwelling place, O LORD of hosts! / My soul
> longs, indeed it faints for the courts of the LORD; my heart and
> my flesh sing for joy to the living God. / Even the sparrow finds
> a home, and the swallow a nest for herself, where she may lay
> her young, at your altars, O LORD of hosts . . . / For the LORD
> God is a sun and shield; he bestows favor and honor. No good

thing does the LORD withhold from those who walk uprightly. / O LORD of hosts, happy is everyone who trusts in you. (Psalm 84:1-3, 11-12)

### Prayer

Living God, Loving God, in awe of this new life, and in gratitude, Linda and Jim receive this child. Their hearts and the hearts of their families are full. How long they have waited to know this baby! To hold her and cherish her! They humbly and gratefully receive this gift, this beautiful child. We ask for peace for the very courageous birth mother who, out of her love, gave them her child to raise and love.

Loving Father, Loving Mother, give Jim and Linda an abundance of grace to parent this blessed life in love, much wisdom for nurture and growth as a family, and strength for this journey into parenthood; in Jesus' name. Amen.

# 6. Premature Infant

### Scripture

For it was you who formed my inward parts; you knit me together in my mother's womb. / I praise you, for I am fearfully and wonderfully made. / How weighty to me are your thoughts, O God! How vast is the sum of them! / I try to count them— they are more than the sand; I come to the end—I am still with you. (Psalm 139:13-14a, 17-18)

### Prayer

God of the weak and vulnerable as well as the mighty, we give you thanks for the birth of baby Noah, even as he struggles to make his way before his time. We pray for his continued development and gaining of strength under the good care of the medical staff here. I lift up these new parents, Jake and Margie, that your guidance and love will be their foundation in the coming days and weeks. May his early birth be a sign of his eagerness for life and his passion for justice and compassion.

Give this family the rest and patience they all need to endure this trial, and let them feel your loving hand holding them close. We pray in the name of the one who welcomed the little children unto himself, Jesus our Lord, who taught us to pray: Our Father who art in heaven...

## 7. Baby Who Is Hospitalized

### *Scripture*

> Sing to the LORD with thanksgiving; make melody to our God on the lyre. / He covers the heavens with clouds, prepares rain for the earth, makes grass grow on the hills. / He gives to the animals their food, and to the young ravens when they cry. / His delight is not in the strength of the horse, nor his pleasure in the speed of a runner; / but the LORD takes pleasure in those who fear him, in those who hope in his steadfast love. (Psalm 147:7-11)

### *Prayer*

Loving God, we pray that you hold baby Jillian in your healing hands, and fill her with your love and grace in this time of illness. Bless this mother, Jill; and bless Zach and his dad, William, who are managing at home while the girls are here. Thank you for the sensitive care of the medical team, and the outpouring of support from family and friends. We know it is your will for health and wholeness for all your creatures; may that come soon for this child. For we ask it in Jesus' name. Amen.

## 8. Child Who Is Hospitalized

### *Scripture*

> I do not cease to give thanks for you as I remember you in my prayers. I pray that the God of our Lord Jesus Christ, the Father of glory, may give you a spirit of wisdom and revelation as you come to know him, so that, with the eyes of your heart enlightened, you may know what is the hope to which he has called you, what are the riches of his glorious inheritance among the

saints, and what is the immeasurable greatness of his power for us who believe, according to the working of his great power. (Ephesians 1:16-19)

### Prayer with the Child

Dear God, I thank you for Andrew being my friend and your friend. I pray for his healing, so that soon he will be feeling better and able to go home after this surgery. He is so blessed to have a great mother in Leda, and for his grandmother and other family and friends who are caring about him through this. Help him be brave through the shots and medicines he has to take, and give him patience and a good spirit to bring joy to the nurses and aides who tend to him. Guide him as he studies the Bible he received from the church, to understand its ways and to live in the light of Jesus, in whose name we pray. Amen.

## 9. Youth Hospitalized for Drug Treatment and Afraid to Face Parents

### Scripture

In you, O LORD, I seek refuge; do not let me ever be put to shame; in your righteousness deliver me. / Incline your ear to me; rescue me speedily. Be a rock of refuge for me, a strong fortress to save me. / You are indeed my rock and my fortress; for your name's sake lead me and guide me, take me out of the net that is hidden for me, for you are my refuge. / Into your hand I commit my spirit. (Psalm 31:1-5a)

### Prayer

Holy God, I pray your blessings upon Jeremy, who has acknowledged his wrong choices that led him to be here in the hospital. Help him talk to his family, for he is so afraid to share his actions that have caused so much pain. We know he is worried that his family will not love him. Help him to know, O God, that you will never abandon him, and that there are many people who will walk this road with him.

Guide him to your side, Mother God, and keep him under your care. Grant Jeremy the courage to tell his family what he has done wrong and ask their forgiveness. Open his heart to accept, with humility, your grace and forgiveness, which are offered through the sacrifice of Christ and leads to new life. Give grace, understanding, and support to his family that they may stand with him in the coming days.

We pray for your healing power to cleanse his body and keep him free from the desire to turn again to drugs. For in you is power to overcome and begin again. We thank you in Jesus' name. Amen.

## 10. Youth Who Is Unlikely to Recover

### Scripture

> Therefore, since we are justified by faith, we have peace with God through our Lord Jesus Christ, through whom we have obtained access to this grace in which we stand; and we boast in our hope of sharing the glory of God. And not only that, but we also boast in our sufferings, knowing that suffering produces endurance, and endurance produces character, and character produces hope, and hope does not disappoint us, because God's love has been poured into our hearts through the Holy Spirit that has been given to us. (Romans 5:1-5)

### Prayer

Guardian God, we proclaim that you are almighty and unchanging, and your mercy knows no limits. You are the God of all ages. We come to you holding fast to the promises that keep us going. We call on your hand of comfort to be present in this situation. We claim your wisdom in all things where our knowledge falls short. God, only you know the future and you know our needs. No matter the length of our days on earth, you sustain us.

In these days of confusion, uncertainty, and pain we pray for your strength to work through this young mind and heart, making yourself evident, that Calvin may be drawn to you. We place the worries of this day at your feet, remembering that the hope you give in eternal life transcends our present pain. We thank you for your saving love and give you praise for the ways you are already at work here and now. In the name of our Savior, Jesus Christ, we pray. Amen.

# RELATED TO DYING AND DEATH

## 1. Longing to Die

### Scripture

> Save me, O God, for the waters have come up to my neck. / I sink in deep mire, where there is no foothold; I have come into deep waters, and the flood sweeps over me. / I am weary with my crying; my throat is parched. My eyes grow dim waiting for my God. / With your faithful help rescue me from sinking in the mire. (Psalm 69:1-3, 13c-14a)

### Prayer

O God of grace and love, you know the distress of Viola's heart, of how she longs to be released from the constant pain and dark shadows that overwhelm her. It is her constant prayer that the passage from death to new life comes quickly. Yet she lingers on and on, sinking into deeper waters. In the midst of this we cry out for the grace of your loving spirit to sustain her. Grant her your peace in heart and mind, body and soul. Your ways are not our ways. Be very near as she journeys through this trial. However you see fit, grant her healing. For we ask it through Christ our Savior. Amen.

## 2. Negative Prognosis

### Scripture

> What then are we to say about these things? If God is for us, who is against us? He who did not withhold his own Son, but gave him up for all of us, will he not with him also give us everything else? . . . Who will separate us from the love of

Christ? Will hardship, or distress, or persecution, or famine, or nakedness, or peril, or sword?... No, in all these things we are more than conquerors through him who loved us. For I am convinced that neither death, nor life, nor angels, nor rulers, nor things present, nor things to come, nor powers, nor height, nor depth, nor anything else in all creation, will be able to separate us from the love of God in Christ Jesus our Lord. (Romans 8:31-32, 35, 37-39)

### Prayer

Merciful God, you are the source of our lives and have loved us from the first day until now. We remember, with deep thankfulness, your faithfulness to us in every season. You have walked beside us in all our days. In times of light and joy, in times of struggle and heartache, in times of success and strength, and in times of darkness and weakness, you have been our comfort and friend and savior. In every season, you have been the source of an unquenchable hope that fortifies our determination and endurance. You have taught us that we are surrounded by an unfathomable love, from which nothing in heaven or on earth will ever be able to separate us.

So now, in this time of serious illness, Emily gives herself into your care and keeping. We ask your continued guidance for the dedicated doctors and nurses, that they may use their gifts of medical skill and human compassion well. We thank you for all her loved ones—family and friends and neighbors—to whom she is bound in unbreakable friendship through these days. We know that whether healing will come in this season or whether it is her time to return to your house of safekeeping and peace, she will always be your beloved child. In this time of human fragileness, help her not be afraid, for your perfect love drives out all fear. We rejoice in you, Lord, and trust our every day and every hour to your safekeeping and mercy. Through Jesus Christ our Lord, we pray. Amen.

## 3. Does Not Have Long to Live

### Scripture

Jesus said to her, "I am the resurrection and the life. Those who believe in me, even though they die, will live, and everyone who lives and believes in me will never die. Do you believe this?" She said to him, "Yes, Lord, I believe that you are the Messiah, the Son of God, the one coming into the world." (John 11:25-27)

### Prayer

Merciful God, our Savior, Lord, and Friend, you who watched in love the death of your beloved Son, and for whom not a single sparrow falls to the ground without your tender notice; we commend ourselves to your grace and care in this hour. You are the Creator who gave us life in the beginning. You are the living God who has walked beside us on the plains, on the mountaintops, and in the valleys of darkness. And now, in this time of our greatest human fragileness, you remain our faithful companion. You, Lord, are the hope of the whole world and of us here in this time and place.

We know that our lives have bounds and that our days are numbered. We know that, in your goodness, you have destined us all to return to your home of safekeeping and peace. No one knows the exact day or hour of our return to your incomparable love and care. But we know that nothing shall ever separate us from the great love that you have made ours in Christ Jesus our Lord. We understand that in this hour, in all the hours that yet follow, and in the life beyond our earthly sojourn, we shall be surrounded by a love that passes all human understanding.

Now into your faithful love and mercy, we commend your daughter Trudy. Just as you stand with us in the hour of our death, we pray that we may stand with you in the hour of the resurrection that you have brought in Christ. May your perfect love cleanse our hearts of any fear. May your joy be our path. And may we be filled with great thankfulness; through Jesus Christ our Lord. Amen.

## 4. When Death Is Imminent

### Scripture

"Do not let your hearts be troubled. Believe in God, believe also in me. In my Father's house there are many dwelling

places. If it were not so, would I have told you that I go to prepare a place for you? And if I go and prepare a place for you, I
will come again and will take you to myself, so that where I am,
there you may be also. And you know the way to the place
where I am going." Thomas said to him, "Lord, we do not know
where you are going. How can we know the way?" Jesus said to
him, "I am the way, and the truth, and the life. No one comes
to the Father except through me. If you know me, you will
know my Father also. From now on you do know him and have
seen him." (John 14:1-7)

### Prayer

Eternal and merciful God, we are joined together around the
deathbed of our beloved relative and friend, Helen. Words are
hard for us as we are compelled to face the reality of a painful and
unanticipated loss of one with whom we shared many years of life
and wonderful experience. Help us learn to find ways to fill the
emptiness we feel, to bear the burden of grief that will be our companion in the days ahead, and to discover anew the assurance that
the awareness of your comforting presence makes ever possible.

Enable us, Loving Master, to know in new ways, the beauty
and wonder of the family that has nurtured us and brought mul-
tiple blessings to us through our pain and our joys. Draw us ever
closer to one another when the night comes, as it has in this
moment. When our confidence is threatened, when we feel vulnerable and alone, help us turn to those closest to us who will
bear us up "lest we dash our feet against a stone."

Speak to us again through the power of your spirit as you, O
God, have done so many times in this family; in the special
moments of trial and need that we have known. Help us to hear
again the words that come to us across the years—that identify
the legacy that is our church—"God is with us." May we be
blessed by the memories of that legacy to withstand whatever trials we must experience, even the great loss that death has visited
upon this family.

Hear us, gracious God, in the name, and for the sake, of our
Savior, who promised that all who believed in him would never

know the sting of death but would feel the power of life eternally and in abundance. Accept this prayer for the sake of Christ and we shall be forever thankful. Amen.

## 5. Prayer over a Stillborn Infant

### Scripture

> Then I saw a new heaven and a new earth; ... And I heard a loud voice from the throne saying,
> "See, the home of God is among mortals. He will dwell with them as their God; they will be his peoples, / he will wipe every tear from their eyes. Death will be no more; mourning and crying and pain will be no more, for the first things have passed away." (Revelation 21:1a, 3a, 4)

*It would be appropriate to anoint the child with oil, making the sign of the cross on the baby's forehead during the doxology at the end of the prayer, while being held in the parent's arms.*

### Prayer

We commend the spirit of this precious child into your arms, Loving God. We imagine a great cloud of witnesses, this mother and father's ancestors and all the saints of earth who now abide with you. May their loving arms receive this cherished baby, Karen, providing her with all the love we ache to give. We pray in the name of God, the creator of life, Jesus, the healer of broken hearts, and the Holy Spirit, who abides with us always. Amen.

## 6. Family Members Unable to Say Good-bye to Loved One Before Death

### Scripture

> What then are we to say about these things? If God is for us, who is against us? He who did not withhold his own Son, but gave him up for all of us, will he not with him also give us

everything else? Who will bring any charge against God's elect? It is God who justifies. Who is to condemn? It is Christ Jesus, who died, yes, who was raised, who is at the right hand of God, who indeed intercedes for us. Who will separate us from the love of Christ? Will hardship, or distress, or persecution, or famine, or nakedness, or peril, or sword? ... No, in all these things we are more than conquerors through him who loved us. For I am convinced that neither death, nor life, nor angels, nor rulers, nor things present, nor things to come, nor powers, nor height, nor depth, nor anything else in all creation, will be able to separate us from the love of God in Christ Jesus our Lord. (Romans 8:31-35, 37-39)

### Prayer

Here we are with Randal, Vera, Ryan, and Lindsay in their grief. To the mysteries of death and the pain of loss are added the anguish of not having had a chance to say good-bye to Olive; the missed opportunities to say whatever was left to be said, to bless and receive a blessing. While we trust that Olive has already been received and made whole in your shining presence, we are left with all the sorry gaps in our timing and in our hearts, with our longings and failings, with our questions.

We thank you that your arms are big enough, your embrace wide enough, and your love powerful enough to bridge all distances, to hold us all close together even now. Draw near in compassion to the Sheets family that they may receive your peace and, in time, be comforted. We pray in the hope and in the name of the one who said, "I will not leave you desolate," even our Lord Jesus the Christ. Amen.

# 7. Surviving Family Who Lost Loved Ones in the Same Accident

### Scripture

My God, my God, why have you forsaken me? Why are you so far from helping me, from the words of my groaning? / I am poured out like water, and all my bones are out of joint; my heart is like wax, it is melted within my breast ... / But you, O LORD, do not be far away! O my help, come quickly to my aid! (Psalm 22:1, 14, 19)

### Prayer

Dear Heavenly Lord, it is so hard to bear the pain of this hour. Our hearts are breaking, we are numb, we are angry, and we are completely at a loss. No words are adequate; we are outside of anything we recognize as normal life. I ask your blessing on this family, and on Ron and Rhonda here with me now. I cannot imagine their pain at the loss of their children but I sense their real need for your touch.

We know of your love, we have long heard of it, and as difficult as it is to comprehend this terrible event, we look to you as a companion in grief. For Ron and Rhonda, I ask your special blessing. May the comfort of your Son Jesus, his tender love, human and divine, come into this room. I pray in Christ's name. Amen.

## 8. Family Whose Loss Was Due to Suicide

### Scripture

> For I am convinced that neither death, nor life, nor angels, nor rulers, nor things present, nor things to come, nor powers, nor height, nor depth, nor anything else in all creation, will be able to separate us from the love of God in Christ Jesus our Lord. (Romans 8:38-39)

### Prayer

God of hope, our light in the darkness, we know that nothing can separate us from your love through Christ Jesus our Lord. We ask you to sustain us with your strength as we mourn the passing of Stanley. O God, you know the demons and despair that haunted him in this world. We pray that he is now at peace in your perfect care. We grieve, Lord, that our arms were unable to catch Stanley when he encountered such despair. Forgive us where we fell short; forgive him for feeling that there was nowhere else to turn. We trust that he has found a safe haven in your everlasting arms.

Loving God, we ask that your comforting hand rest on those of us who loved Stanley. Though our questions of "why?" and "what could we have done?" may go unanswered, we pray that your peace, which passes all understanding, will reign in our hearts until the day we join our brother in your heavenly kingdom, where death and despair have no power. In the name of your redeeming Son, Jesus Christ, and the power of your Holy Spirit we pray. Amen.

# RELATED TO ACCIDENT OR VIOLENCE

## 1. Injured Due to Street Violence

### Scripture

Do not repay anyone evil for evil, but take thought for what is noble in the sight of all. If it is possible, so far as it depends on you, live peaceably with all. Beloved, never avenge yourselves, but leave room for the wrath of God ... Do not be overcome by evil, but overcome evil with good. (Romans 12:17-19a, 21)

### Prayer

Dear God, Comforter and Advocate, be with us as we stand here beside the bed of Daniel, our friend, who has need for the touch of your healing hand. Give him strength to bear the hurt that has come upon him and restore his body and soul. We are angry and sad at the random and violent manner in which he was hurt. We are called to be your peacemakers but our hearts are angry at what has happened. This violence has reached out and touched our friend and brother, and brought him to this need for healing, and we grieve with him in his pain.

Be with Daniel and heal the damage done to his body. Be with him and with us too, as we struggle with our desire to exact revenge. Help us leave our anger behind. Do not let us carry it back to the streets. Help us to forgive those who had a part in hurting our friend. Those who did this acted out of their own trouble and pain. Help them to know what they have done and move them to repentance. Touch their souls too, in a way that will restore peace.

Give us strength to mirror your love and not our anger to those we meet. Fashion us in your image so that we may bear suffering with grace and be your instrument for peace. Give us strength and forgive us where we fail. Be with all who suffer in a world where violence lies so close to the surface of our lives. Give us your peace. In your Son's name we ask all this. Amen.

# 2. Injured Due to Natural Disaster

### Scripture

> Blessed be the God and Father of our Lord Jesus Christ! By his great mercy he has given us a new birth into a living hope through the resurrection of Jesus Christ from the dead . . . In this you rejoice, even if now for a little while you have had to suffer various trials, so that the genuineness of your faith— being more precious than gold that, though perishable, is tested by fire—may be found to result in praise and glory and honor when Jesus Christ is revealed. (1 Peter 1:3, 6-7)

### Prayer

God of hopes and dreams, we do not understand the ways of this world. We do not understand why natural disasters happen. Yet, even in our lack of understanding, we know that you are present with us. You are here amid the devastation and loss. We come to you, asking for your strength and your love to be with Kathy, as she has lost the place that she and Russ call home. They worked so hard to make it a place of relaxation and refreshment, of hospitality and memories. Help her to see the promises that are found in you, through your grace and your mercy. Help them both to move through their grief and have the strength to rebuild again when they feel it is time. In the meantime, strengthen her and aid her recovery from this tragedy. We pray all this in the name of the one Christ who is with us in trouble and despair. Amen.

# 3. Rape Victim

## Scripture

[God] gives power to the faint, and strengthens the powerless. / Even youths will faint and be weary, and the young will fall exhausted; / but those who wait for the LORD shall renew their strength, they shall mount up with wings like eagles, they shall run and not be weary, they shall walk and not faint. (Isaiah 40:29-31)

## Prayer

Ever present, ever tender, ever compassionate God, we confess that there are no words to explain this hideous and painful crime committed against the will and innocence of Lisa. Our souls scream out, "why?" We know this is not your will because you beckon us to help and protect the weak and the vulnerable. You are a God of love, who would never willingly grieve or afflict your children. Even now we see your care for Lisa in the face of every caring professional. These "Good Samaritans," though strangers, have stopped whatever else they were doing to perform your work of comfort, treatment, and healing.

We sense now your special nearness with Lisa. We know that even though we cannot understand the meanness of others, you understand the suffering it has caused. Like your son, Jesus who was physically beaten and shamed publicly on the cross, this precious daughter has been brutally offended through no fault of her own. May your promise of new life and hope, extended to us in Christ's victory over sin and death, transform this hour of agony so that Lisa might be healed in body, mind, and spirit. Then may she find courage and peace again in the love and support of family and friends. Renew her strength to "mount up with wings like eagles" to rise above this tragedy. And always we pray for that day "on earth, as it is in heaven" when your daughters and sons will walk unafraid in a world of peace and justice. Amen.

# 4. Victim of Domestic Violence

### Scripture

> Give ear to my words, O LORD; give heed to my sighing. / Listen to the sound of my cry, / For you are not a God who delights in wickedness; evil will not sojourn with you. / Lead me, O LORD, in your righteousness because of my enemies; make your way straight before me. / Make them bear their guilt, O God; let them fall by their own counsels. / But let all who take refuge in you rejoice; let them ever sing for joy. (Psalm 5:1-2a, 4, 8, 10a, 11a)

### Prayer

God of new beginnings, help Nancy to know that you are the source of healing, love, and mercy. She is hurt in so many ways; it is hard to know where to look for comfort. Help her to feel that you are the source of comfort and security. Give her the strength to seek comfort through your love.

Bring your healing power to Nancy's body, mind, and spirit. Keep her children safe in the care of her parents as she recovers. Bring justice so that this will not happen again. We thank you for revealing to her the wrong that has been done to her, and for helping her take steps to share the truth. Compassionate God, help her to know that she is worthy of receiving your love and the love of others. Grant her peace that is found in the love we know through Christ our Lord. Amen.

# 5. Injury Due to War

### Scripture

> Recalling your tears, I long to see you so that I may be filled with joy. I am reminded of your sincere faith, a faith that lived first in your grandmother Lois and your mother Eunice and now, I am sure, lives in you. For this reason I remind you to rekindle the gift of God that is within you through the laying

on of my hands; for God did not give us a spirit of cowardice, but rather a spirit of power and of love and of self-discipline. (2 Timothy 1:4-7)

### Prayer

God of Justice and Mercy, we pray for Mike at this time, knowing how much you love him, and how difficult this situation is. We thank you for the understanding of service that led him to give himself in this way, but we also confess how hard it is to see him bear this pain. It strikes us as unfair, for his task was to do good, to help. Mike needs you now, Lord. Allow him to receive your courage and your wisdom in a mighty way. Relieve him of the nightmares of the horrors of war.

We have every hope in your healing power, and yet we also ask directly: Bring him out of this somehow. Move him to a new place in his life. Give him strength of body, mind, and spirit. We ask your blessing on Mike's family, his friends, and especially those of his comrades who continue to be in harm's way. Bring us all to the peace that passes understanding. In Christ's name we pray. Amen.

# RELATED TO SPECIAL CIRCUMSTANCES

## 1. New Immigrant Who Has Fallen Ill

### Scripture

Seek the LORD while he may be found, call upon him while he is near; / For as the heavens are higher than the earth, so are my ways higher than your ways and my thoughts than your thoughts.

... And the foreigners who join themselves to the LORD, to minister to him, to love the name of the LORD, and to be his servants, all who keep the sabbath, and do not profane it, and hold fast my covenant— / these I will bring to my holy mountain, and make them joyful in my house of prayer. (Isaiah 55:6, 9; 56:6-7a)

## Prayer

God of Abraham and Sarah, God of pilgrims, you are the God of Young-Mee too. We thank you for leading Young-Mee and her family to this land, accompanying her with your abiding presence in every bend of her journey. She is now in need of your healing and comforting presence. Give her health and strength, fill her with your courage and faith, so that she may resume work and continue to pursue her dreams without fear, without doubt.

O God, you are the source of life and salvation. Grant hope and protection to Young-Mee, and all the immigrants in this land; sustain and renew them in their struggle to find the right road in their lives. We are grateful for the freedoms we know in this land; help us all live in ways that strengthen the common good and build strong community. Teach us to live in the way of Jesus Christ, in whose name we pray. Amen.

# 2. Recent Refugee

## Scripture

> For the LORD your God is God of gods and LORD of lords, . . . who is not partial and takes no bribe, who executes justice for the orphan and the widow, and who loves the strangers, providing them food and clothing. You shall also love the stranger, for you were strangers in the land of Egypt. You shall fear the LORD your God; him alone you shall worship; to him you shall hold fast. (Deuteronomy 10:17-20b)

## Prayer

Sovereign God, who took on the very form of a servant, lived as a refugee on earth, and was humbled through death on a cross, watch over Humberto, your suffering child. He has been led along a path of trial, tribulation, suffering, and sorrow: losing home, family, country, and property. Touch him with your powerful grace, bring healing and peace, restore hope and a future. Be closer than a brother to him, soothe and bind his broken heart, heal and help his aching flesh. May that same resurrection power that lifted Christ from the very grave, fill and renew this your son so that your life, light, love, and provision may be plain to see—for him, in him, and through him. We ask it in the name of Christ. Amen.

# 3. College Student

### Scripture

My child, if you accept my words and treasure up my commandments within you, / making your ear attentive to wisdom and inclining your heart to understanding; / if you indeed cry out for insight, and raise your voice for understanding; / if you seek it like silver, and search for it as for hidden treasures— / then you will understand the fear of the LORD and find the knowledge of God. For the LORD gives wisdom; from his mouth come knowledge and understanding; / he stores up sound wisdom for the upright; he is a shield to those who walk blamelessly, / guarding the paths of justice and preserving the way of his faithful ones. (Proverbs 2:1-8)

### Prayer

O Holy One, I thank you for the sunshine of this day that reminds us of both your warmth and light. I am grateful for Betsy, and for the joy she has known and brought to our campus—through celebrations and parades, her joy and laughter. I pray you would be with her and give her comfort in this time of illness. Relieve her anxiety about uncompleted papers and studies and let her simply rest in you. Help her to know the compassion and understanding of teachers, family, and friends who will help her through this time. May she draw near to you and, in so doing, find truth, understanding, and hope.

I ask you to be present with each of us in those places where we need grace, where we need healing, where we need strength. Guide all that we say and do so that our work and our lives will make a positive difference in our corner of the world. Help Betsy shine with warmth and light to all who care for her, that healing may come in body and spirit. This I pray in the name of the one who is holy, Jesus the Christ. Amen.

# 4. Suffering Depression

### Scripture

> For this reason I bow my knees before the Father, from whom every family in heaven and on earth takes its name. I pray that, according to the riches of his glory, he may grant that you may be strengthened in your inner being with power through his Spirit, and that Christ may dwell in your hearts through faith, as you are being rooted and grounded in love. I pray that you may have the power to comprehend, with all the saints, what is the breadth and length and height and depth, and to know the love of Christ that surpasses knowledge, so that you may be filled with all the fullness of God. (Ephesians 3:14-19)

### Prayer

Holy Intimate God, source of all healing and hope, we pray for Randy and all those suffering from depression. As he journeys through a land of deep darkness, bring the light of your grace into his life so he may have clarity of thought and emotion. Heal his mind and heart from the pain that haunts him and ease the burden he feels.

Free Randy from the hurt of the past and the shame that separates him from the love of others and help him to know and trust that his life is valued, wanted, and needed for your purposes. Give patience and understanding to Gayle and their loved ones and friends so that, together, they may hold each other up when darkness would make them stumble. We pray in the name of Jesus, who died and entered all our darkness so we may rise to new life in the light of his presence, now and in the kingdom yet to come. Amen.

36

# 5. Patient Who Also Has Alzheimer's

### Scripture

> The LORD is my shepherd; I shall not want. / He maketh me to lie down in green pastures: he leadeth me beside the still waters. He restoreth my soul. (Psalm 23:1-3a, KJV)

### Prayer

Eternal Light who guides our way, we pray for Loraine as she is hospitalized. But Lord, we also know she has Alzheimer's. It has robbed her of past and future and of her way with words. She no longer recognizes her husband and son, and that is hard on them. They no longer like to visit. But Loraine has moments, Lord, moments when she sings, or when she smiles, or when she "mouths" the Lord's Prayer, or when she holds hands in her former mothering way. Those moments are precious, Lord. Thank you for such gifts in these times. Let her family come to enjoy them.

We are unsure of how to ask for healing. We trust your wisdom and compassion that will bring her to that place where there is no more suffering. I thank you that I can be present with her and represent your love for her. It is in Jesus' name we pray. Amen.

# 6. Enduring Painful Rehabilitation

### Scripture

> The wilderness and the dry land shall be glad, the desert shall rejoice and blossom ... / Strengthen the weak hands, and make firm the feeble knees. / Say to those who are of a fearful heart, "Be strong, do not fear!" / they shall obtain joy and gladness, and sorrow and sighing shall flee away. (Isaiah 35:1, 3-4a, 10b)

### Prayer

Dear Patient and Renewing God, Nell, my friend here, is in a panic this afternoon. She is shaking and her eyes are red from tears. She is holding my hands very tight. The doctors have explained their recommended treatment and she is scared to death. She is afraid of the unknown, of the pain, and the uncertainty of the outcome. Rehabilitation is difficult work.

I pray that your healing Spirit may be here—now. Come be with us. Like a breath of fresh air, take away her anxiety and assure her of your steadfast presence. Relax Nell's body and fill her with the calmness of your spirit. Give her strength to work hard, to look beyond the pain to the day when her recovery will enable her to function as she once did. Keep us both in your love and care, for we pray in Jesus' name. Amen.

# 7. Facing a Long Recovery

### Scripture

> We are afflicted in every way, but not crushed; perplexed, but not driven to despair; persecuted, but not forsaken; struck down, but not destroyed. (2 Corinthians 4:8-9)

### Prayer

Well, God, we have to tell you, Dan had prepared himself for the fear and stress of this illness. We had an idea of how long this was going to last and he knew he could get through it. Then the whole picture changed and he must prepare in a new way. We do not know when there will be relief for him. Most of all, he and Chris are scared, but must be feeling helpless and angry too. Dan is not himself—his strength, his capabilities—all are diminished. His partner worries about having enough to give him. How long will this last?

God, we need your help. Please hear our prayer. Grant healing and hope. Give Chris an attitude of selflessness; give Dan patience. Help them move through this time in their lives with grace and love toward each other. Thank you for your words of promise in Matthew 11, "Come to me, all you who labor and are heavy laden, and I will give you rest." All these things I ask in Jesus' name. Amen.

# 8. Farmers Anxious about Crops and Animals

### Scripture

You then, my child, be strong in the grace that is in Christ Jesus; and what you have heard from me through many witnesses entrust to faithful people who will be able to teach others as well. Share in suffering like a good soldier of Christ Jesus. No one serving in the army gets entangled in everyday affairs; the soldier's aim is to please the enlisting officer... It is the farmer who does the work who ought to have the first share of the crops. (2 Timothy 2:1-4, 6)

### Prayer

O God, Farmer of our lives and Grower of all that nurtures us, hold the hand of Roy, who has grown flocks and crops as your trustworthy steward, and has seen your blessing like the sunshine on produce. Tend your lamb, Roy, with your loving care and healing hand as he suffers. Give rest and restore his strength.

Please bring forth those who can take over his labor on the farm and continue the work. Help him always to entrust his life to your powerful and always available strength. We pray, relying on the care of our Good Shepherd, Jesus Christ. Amen.

# 9. Hospitalized while Incarcerated

### Scripture

Where can I go from your spirit? Or where can I flee from your presence? / If I ascend to heaven, you are there; if I make my bed in Sheol, you are there. / If I say, "Surely the darkness shall cover me, and the light around me become night," / even the darkness is not dark to you; the night is as bright as the day, for darkness is as light to you. (Psalm 139:7-8, 11-12)

**Prayer**

God of light and life, your presence knows no boundaries and penetrates our deepest darkness. Your spirit breaks through all the walls that separate us from abundant life. You know our deepest longings for healing and health, forgiveness and restoration, freedom and love. Help Nathan to know your loving and healing presence in the midst of his weakness and confinement. May the awareness of your presence and the assurance of your love be light in our darkness, strength in our weakness, freedom in our confinement, hope amid our discouragement.

Enable Nathan to claim the promise that "the light shines in the darkness and the darkness cannot overcome it." In the name of Jesus Christ, who is the light of the world, we pray. Amen.

# 10. Someone Unconscious

*Remember that someone who is unresponsive may actually be able to hear and understand us. Singing a familiar hymn or praying the Lord's Prayer may be especially comforting.*

**Scripture**

So [Naomi] said, "See, your sister-in-law has gone back to her people and to her gods; return after your sister-in-law." But Ruth said,

"Do not press me to leave you or to turn back from following you! Where you go, I will go; where you lodge, I will lodge; your people shall be my people and your God my God. / Where you die, I will die—there will I be buried. May the LORD do thus and so to me, and more as well, if even death parts me from you!"

When Naomi saw that she was determined to go with her, she said no more to her. (Ruth 1:15-18)

**Prayer**

God in whom we live and move and have our being, I thank you that your grace and mercy surround us like light, that your spirit moves in us like breath, that your resurrection power is a song sung into our bones.

Bathe this brother Gregory in your healing grace. Let your wings of mercy shelter him; let him rest in the love that over and around us lies; let him rest in your peace that passes all understanding; let him rest in your joy inexpressible; let him rest in the hands of Jesus.

We pray for your will to be done, and ask for your healing power that will give Gregory release from this captive state. If it must not pass, then grant him your grace to endure and cling to the hope that leads to life everlasting. We pray in Jesus' name, as he taught us, saying, "Our Father, who art in heaven..." Amen.

# 11. Developmentally Disabled Patient

### Scripture

> I will bless the LORD at all times; his praise shall continually be in my mouth. / O magnify the LORD with me, and let us exalt his name together. / I sought the LORD, and he answered me, and delivered me from all my fears. (Psalm 34:1, 3-4)

### Prayer

Dear Lord, I want to thank you for my friend Olaf who is here in the hospital. I am grateful for his presence in my life. Through Olaf I have been given a perspective of the world that I would not otherwise have had. He is a blessing to all who meet him.

We pray for Olaf today, that all that is going on around him will not overwhelm him. We pray for the doctors and nurses, for the treatment recommended, and pray that he will be able to overcome this illness and any and all obstacles that come his way. Give him the confidence he needs and help him spread the joy he brings to the many hospital staff members who tend to him. Lord, please open the hearts and minds of each individual who comes in contact with Olaf throughout the day. Help others see him through your eyes with all that make him the special person that he is. Allow them to see his gifts, and honor them.

Lord, hold Olaf in love and protect him from the ills and discrimination of the world. May your healing be manifest in him and your love present with him. We pray through Jesus Christ our Lord. Amen.

# 12. Attempted Suicide (Prayer with Family Present)

### Scripture

> Where can I go from your spirit? Or where can I flee from your presence? / If I ascend to heaven, you are there; if I make my bed in Sheol, you are there. / If I say, "Surely the darkness shall cover me, and the light around me become night," / even the darkness is not dark to you; the night is as bright as the day, for darkness is as light to you. (Psalm 139:7-8, 11-12)

### Prayer

Great God of life, we give you thanks for our loved one, Regina. We thank you for her portion of joy on her pilgrimage with us. We bless you, O Lord, for every touch of hers that has shaped us and formed our friendships, and for her unique gifts on which we have depended. We pray for her now, especially the despair that oppressed her and the deep agony that overtook her and led her to this desperate act. Our hearts are heavy with her brokenness. Please forgive us for our inability to keep this from happening, please free us from the regret we feel that we did not do more, that our interactions were not enough.

Grant us all healing and wholeness. Give Regina the strength she needs as she struggles back to purpose and joy, and guide us all toward lives that serve you and others. We pray in Jesus' name. Amen.

# 13. Psychotic Patient

### Scripture

Hear, O LORD, when I cry aloud, be gracious to me and answer me! / "Come," my heart says, "seek his face!" Your face, LORD, do I seek. / Do not hide your face from me. / Wait for the LORD; be strong, and let your heart take courage; wait for the LORD! (Psalm 27:7-9a, 14)

### Prayer

O God, God, God; Jill is back. She is cowered in the corner here, frightened and frightening to others. While she hunkers down, suspiciously scanning all that happens around her, she hears this nagging voice—"Jill, Jill, Jill"—a mean and judgmental voice beckoning her to hurt herself. She thinks that hurting herself is payment due for being a bad person. God, let Jill know that she is a good person, that you love her just as she is. Let Jill know that these voices are not real voices. Let her hear our voices instead, and those of the hospital staff; real voices that want to help her find herself, find you, and find healing. Speak through us as your servants, as we bring genuine concern and medications, challenge to choose the right path, and comfort for her journey back to wholeness. Grant her the peace of Jesus Christ, in whose name we pray. Amen.

# RELATED TO PERSONAL CONCERNS OF THE PATIENT

## 1. Worried about a Child Deployed in the Military

### Scripture

The LORD is my rock, my fortress, and my deliverer, / my God, my rock, in whom I take refuge, my shield and the horn of my salvation, my stronghold and my refuge, my savior; you save me from violence. / I call upon the LORD, who is worthy to be praised, and I am saved from my enemies. (2 Samuel 22:2b-4)

### Prayer

We come before you God, who is called both the Prince of Peace and the Lord of Hosts. In moments like these we recognize that life is not within our control. Marian's body is sick and weak. Her child is in a place of conflict and violence. In many ways both of them feel close to death. We pray for life and we pray for peace.

Help us to understand in our bones that death is not the victor. Help us to know that death does not have the final word. Standing here on death's doorway, thinking of Jeff and others in the military standing watch in the shadow of death, it is so very hard to believe in the resurrection. Help us in our unbelief. Give us courage and perseverance. Give us grace and deliver us from evil. In the name of the one who brings healing and peace, in the name of Jesus Christ, we pray. Amen.

## 2. Worried about Paying the Hospital Bill

### Scripture

"Therefore I tell you, do not worry about your life, what you will eat or what you will drink, or about your body, what you will wear. Is not life more than food, and the body more than clothing? Look at the birds of the air; they neither sow nor reap nor gather into barns, and yet your heavenly Father feeds them. Are you not of more value than they? And can any of you by worrying add a single hour to your span of life? ...

"So do not worry about tomorrow, for tomorrow will bring worries of its own." (Matthew 6:25-27, 34a)

### Prayer

Almighty God, I lift up the concern of your people who are sick and who struggle with worries of how they are going to pay their hospital bills. We especially lift up Letechia, and pray that the day shall come when she and all people will no longer have to worry over such things as bills, finances, food, housing, medical coverage, and the day-to-day matters that make our lives such a struggle.

As Matthew 6 reminds us, help Letechia have no anxiety about the things we need in this world. But Lord, we pray that there will be others to assist in bearing her burdens and helping her through this time of trial. Help her, Lord, grow to trust in your word and become a stronger person of faith. Bring healing to her body and comfort to her soul. Help us understand that you are indeed the supplier of all our needs on earth and in heaven. Hear the cry of your people, "Lord, have mercy on us." In Jesus' name; Amen.

# 3. Wants to Go Home but Cannot

## Scripture

"Do not let your hearts be troubled. Believe in God, believe also in me. In my Father's house there are many dwelling places. If it were not so, would I have told you that I go to prepare a place for you? And if I go and prepare a place for you, I will come again and will take you to myself, so that where I am, there you may be also." (John 14:1-3)

## Prayer

Most Holy God, you are the Ancient of Days, present in all times and places. We come to you now, praying on behalf of John, who so desires to return to his home. Grant him strength for the period of continued recovery and patience to understand your purposes, even in this illness. We pray for all who minister to him here—doctors, nurses, technicians, family, loved ones, and friends—may their every action be an expression of your sustaining grace. Give John your comfort, and may he know the peace from you that passes all understanding; through Christ our Lord. Amen.

# 4. Wants Prayer for Family Members

## Scripture

I have heard of your faith in the Lord Jesus and your love toward all the saints, and for this reason I do not cease to give thanks for you as I remember you in my prayers. I pray that the

God of our Lord Jesus Christ, the Father of glory, may give you a spirit of wisdom and revelation as you come to know him, so that, with the eyes of your heart enlightened, you may know what is the hope to which he has called you, what are the riches of his glorious inheritance among the saints, and what is the immeasurable greatness of his power for us who believe, according to the working of his great power. (Ephesians 1:15-19)

### Prayer

Loving Lord, you are good and your faithfulness continues through all generations. Now, stretch out your hand of mercy, comfort, and peace to Joni's family. May their minds discern your will at work during this time of trial; may their hearts rest through trust in your divine will and power; may their relationships deepen as they depend more upon you and each other; and in this adversity, may their love for you and each other be strengthened through the power of your Holy Spirit. Wrap each one securely in your arms of tender mercy and healing love. We ask it in Jesus' name. Amen.

## 5. Feels Guilty about Surviving an Accident

### Scripture

To you, O LORD, I lift up my soul. / O my God, in you I trust; do not let me be put to shame; do not let my enemies exult over me. / Make me to know your ways, O LORD; teach me your paths. / Turn to me and be gracious to me, for I am lonely and afflicted. / Relieve the troubles of my heart, and bring me out of my distress. (Psalm 25:1-2, 4, 16-17)

### Prayer

Abba, Father, in this dark hour, we simply cry out to you to sustain us. We know you are there but we also know despair, horrifying pain, and loss. Help us all, but especially your child Duane here. He is suffering. We do not know why his brother was killed this evening, and Duane survived, but we know you grieve along with his family, that you know our hurts from the inside.

It is especially hard for Duane. He wonders why this happened; an impossible question, but a real question. We ask that you give him a road to follow, a path in the midst of this dark night. Sustain him moment to moment; allow him to receive the love of those who are so glad he is alive. Bring healing to his body and comfort to his soul. May his purpose for living, when vision becomes clear, strengthen him with new resolve. May your peace, when it comes, find a home in his heart. We pray in Christ's name. Amen.

# 6. Grieving Friends Who Died in the Same Accident

## Scripture

When the poor and needy seek water, and there is none, and their tongue is parched with thirst, I the LORD will answer them, I the God of Israel will not forsake them. / I will open rivers on the bare heights, and fountains in the midst of the valleys; I will make the wilderness a pool of water, and the dry land springs of water. / I will set in the desert the cypress, the plane and the pine together, / so that all may see and know, all may consider and understand, that the hand of the LORD has done this, the Holy One of Israel has created it. (Isaiah 41:17-18, 19b-20)

## Prayer

Guiding Light, who accompanies us in our Lord Jesus Christ, illumine us with your love and presence today, and befriend us through your Holy Spirit. Bless Robin with your healing power, and the assurance of your tender mercies, and the abiding promise of your presence. We do not understand this tragic accident in which Robin's friends died; we do not know why she alone came through. Help her not despair; lead her into renewed life that honors their memory and allows good to come from this.

Help Robin know we are never alone but are always in your care. Grant us your peace through Jesus our Lord, our brother and friend. Remind us of the comfort of your Holy Spirit and help us claim the fellowship of faith with all those who love you. Amen.

# 7. Desires Inner Peace

## Scripture

"I have said these things to you while I am still with you. But the Advocate, the Holy Spirit, whom the Father will send in my name, will teach you everything, and remind you of all that I have said to you. Peace I leave with you; my peace I give to you. I do not give to you as the world gives. Do not let your hearts be troubled, and do not let them be afraid." (John 14:25-27)

## Prayer

Dearest God, Jesus said once that he did not bring peace, but a sword, and sometimes it feels as if that sword is piercing our hearts and will not let us rest. But he also said that he would grant us peace, not peace that the world offers but a peace that comes from God. That is the peace we want, the peace we need: peace from you and peace with you. You know how troubled Valeria is right now. There is no cheap and easy peace for her in this difficult situation; her heart feels pierced with a sword of hurt and sorrow and she is deeply troubled and distressed.

And yet, in the middle of this distress, we ask, with confidence, for what Jesus promised: for the peace which is not like any other, the peace that the Holy Spirit brings, the peace that can help Valeria face this moment—the peace that surpasses all understanding.

Dearest God, we pray that you heal Valeria's sickness, quiet her heart, and allow her to experience your love and your peace in this place today. In the name of the Prince of Peace, our Lord and Savior Jesus Christ, and by the Holy Spirit we pray; Amen.

# 8. Needs Courage to Endure

### Scripture

Finally, be strong in the Lord and in the strength of his power. Put on the whole armor of God, so that you may be able to stand against the wiles of the devil...

Pray in the Spirit at all times in every prayer and supplication. To that end keep alert and always persevere in supplication for all the saints. (Ephesians 6:10-11, 18)

### Prayer

O God, Fire of Love and Strength of Heart, Billy needs your courage to bear up against the pressures and forces that are afflicting him. We pray for his healing during this time in the hospital. We also ask that you fix his aim on a more distant target; help him to keep focused on your love, your strength, your care. Allow his pride to bend so that he may accept the support and help of others, especially his family and friends who care so much for him.

Keep Billy's eyes on the prize, so he can see beyond what is happening now. Fill him with your healing and compassion so there is no room to be anxious. God, keep us all moving toward you, aiming toward your good purpose in our lives. For we pray in Jesus' name. Amen.

# 9. Refuses to Be Comforted

### Scripture

So then, putting away falsehood, let all of us speak the truth to our neighbors, for we are members of one another. Be angry but do not sin; do not let the sun go down on your anger, and do not make room for the devil . . . And do not grieve the Holy Spirit of God, with which you were marked with a seal for the day of redemption. Put away from you all bitterness and wrath and anger and wrangling and slander, together with all malice, and be kind to one another, tenderhearted, forgiving one another, as God in Christ has forgiven you. (Ephesians 4:25-27, 30-32)

### Prayer

Compassionate One, you reach out to us in mercy, understanding the depth of our despair. You hear our silent cries and you see our hidden sorrow. Your promise of comfort and care reaches through the rubble of our lives to find us when we are lost, and you pluck us up even from the bowels of grief. God, we call upon you for Margaret, one who feels lost and alone, who finds it impossible to make the journey to health and wholeness. In your mercy, Lord, grant her the tender care she needs.

Gracious Comforter, reorder the life of your servant Margaret so that, as in creation, your quickening Spirit may take hold and restore light and joy to her soul. Give her hope that she may see her way beyond this illness and hospital stay to renewed life and activity. Let your grace be upon her and grant her your peace. In the name of Jesus Christ our Savior, we pray. Amen.

## 10. Needs Forgiveness while Ill

### Scripture

> Happy are those whose transgression is forgiven, whose sin is covered. / Happy are those to whom the LORD imputes no iniquity, and in whose spirit there is no deceit. / While I kept silence, my body wasted away through my groaning all day long. / For day and night your hand was heavy upon me; my strength was dried up as by the heat of summer. / Then I acknowledged my sin to you, and I did not hide my iniquity; I said, "I will confess my transgressions to the LORD," and you forgave the guilt of my sin. (Psalm 32:1-5)

### Prayer

Generous God, you heal us and make us whole by the power of your presence. You forgive sin and you restore lives from places of brokenness and disease. When our sinful wandering takes us away from you, your love guides us back to the path of righteousness. With justifying grace you reach out to forgive all who turn to you in repentance. We call to you, Holy One, for your child David, who is in need of healing in both body and spirit. Reveal the truth of your forgiving grace in his life. Help him to accept the forgiveness and the love that you offer freely to all who call upon you. Let him claim the new life and the wholeness that you give through the power and presence of your Holy Spirit. Amen.

## 11. Feels Guilty for Being in the Hospital

### Scripture

As God's chosen ones, holy and beloved, clothe yourselves with compassion, kindness, humility, meekness, and patience. Bear with one another and, if anyone has a complaint against another, forgive each other; just as the Lord has forgiven you, so you also must forgive. Above all, clothe yourselves with love, which binds everything together in perfect harmony. And let the peace of Christ rule in your hearts, to which indeed you were called in the one body. And be thankful... And whatever you do, in word or deed, do everything in the name of the Lord Jesus, giving thanks to God the Father through him. (Colossians 3:12-15, 17)

### Prayer

Eternal God, whose mercy is over all you have made, Thelma needs your healing touch. Grant her, in these hours of uncertainty, the assurance of your presence. Her plans are interrupted; help her to trust you for the future. In her infirmity free her from feelings of helplessness and guilt; she does not want to be a burden to others. Ground her faith in the hope that is our strength as Christians. Plant in her the love that transcends our circumstances. Help her to stand in the grace of our faith in Christ Jesus, our Lord. Amen.

# Prayers with Hospital and Nursing Staff

## 1. Hospital Staff Who Feel Overwhelmed

### Scripture

"Ask, and it will be given you; search, and you will find; knock, and the door will be opened for you. For everyone who asks receives, and everyone who searches finds, and for everyone who knocks, the door will be opened . . .

"In everything do to others as you would have them do to you; for this is the law and the prophets." (Matthew 7:7-8, 12)

### Prayer

Dear Lord, please be with this staff as they minister to their patients. Please help them to choose healing words and a gentle touch so that their patients feel your presence and comfort. Through them, may your acceptance and healing power be known as they endure tests, procedures, and surgeries.

Please assist doctors, nurses, technicians, and aides to work as colleagues together, under your guidance, so that we can care, not only for our patients but also for one another. We are your community of caregivers. Please help us feel your presence and give us the wisdom to make good decisions.

Please help hospital management feel your presence and give them the wisdom to live out your ministry. It is difficult at times to make spirit-filled choices in an environment of financial constraints and overwhelming needs. Please help them maintain fiscal solvency as they also live out the hospital mission of serving the human spirit along with the human body. We are here to care for the sick. Please help the administration embody the living mission of your work in their decision-making, communications, and behaviors. These things we ask in the name of the Great Physician, Jesus Christ our Lord. Amen.

## 2. Hospital Staff Experiencing Grief

### Prayer

Loving God, the Source of Wholeness, we give you thanks for this place of healing and these people who do healing work. We are grateful for your wisdom, which works through the medical community to minister to those who are ill; and for the marvelous ways that health comes through surgery, medication, therapy, rest, and care.

Yet Lord, we experience times when these treatments do not work, and our patients fail to thrive, and even die. Why do some respond and heal, and others do not? Why do we lose some patients and not others? Why is it that those to whom we become attached are the ones that sometimes do not make it?

O Holy Healer, we know we should maintain a "professional distance" from all the patients. Yet we also know that you make each of us unique, with our own stories. As we offer care, we come to know some patients through their difficult journeys and through their interest in us. You work through the particular; your incarnational presence requires our involvement.

Comfort us now in the loss of Anne. We give thanks that her suffering is over. We rejoice in her long, committed life and the wonderful support she had from family and friends. Help the staff continue to reach out to our patients and to know, even as we grieve, that your purpose is being worked out in some way through her life and ours.

Bless us now as we continue our work. To those who doubt, give light; to those who are weak, give strength; to all who have sinned, mercy; and to all who sorrow, grant your peace. We ask it in Jesus' name. Amen.

# CHAPTER THREE

---

# HYMNS APPROPRIATE TO SING WITH PATIENTS

## ILL BUT HOPEFUL OF RECOVERY

### There Is a Balm in Gilead
*Refrain*
There is a balm in Gilead
to make the wounded whole;
There is a balm in Gilead
to heal the sin-sick soul.

Sometimes I feel discouraged,
and think my work's in vain.
But then the Holy Spirit
revives my soul again. *Refrain*

If you can't preach like Peter,
if you can't pray like Paul,
Just tell the love of Jesus,
and say he died for all. *Refrain*
—African American spiritual

## Blessed Assurance

Blessed assurance, Jesus is mine!
O what a foretaste of glory divine!
Heir of salvation, purchase of God,
born of his Spirit, washed in his blood.

*Refrain*
This is my story, this is my song,
praising my Savior all the day long;
This is my story, this is my song,
praising my Savior all the day long.

Perfect submission, all is at rest;
I in my Savior am happy and blest,
watching and waiting, looking above,
filled with his goodness, lost in his love. *Refrain*
—Words by Fanny J. Crosby

## Come, Thou Fount of Every Blessing

Come, thou Fount of every blessing,
tune my heart to sing thy grace;
streams of mercy, never ceasing,
call for songs of loudest praise.
Teach me some melodious sonnet,
sung by flaming tongues above.
Praise the mount! I'm fixed upon it,
mount of thy redeeming love.

O to grace how great a debtor
daily I'm constrained to be!
Let thy goodness, like a fetter,
bind my wandering heart to thee.
Prone to wander, Lord, I feel it,
prone to leave the God I love;
here's my heart, O take and seal it,
seal it for thy courts above.
—Words by Robert Robinson

## Wonderful Words of Life

Sing them over again to me,
wonderful words of life;
let me more of their beauty see,
wonderful words of life;
words of life and beauty
teach me faith and duty.

*Refrain*
Beautiful words, wonderful words,
wonderful words of life.
Beautiful words, wonderful words,
wonderful words of life.

Sweetly echo the gospel call,
wonderful words of life;
offer pardon and peace to all,
wonderful words of life;
Jesus, only Savior, sanctify forever. *Refrain*
—Words by Philip P. Bliss

# UNLIKELY TO RECOVER

## On Jordan's Stormy Banks

On Jordan's stormy banks I stand,
and cast a wishful eye
to Canaan's fair and happy land,
where my possessions lie.

*Refrain*
I am bound for the promised land,
I am bound for the promised land;
oh, who will come and go with me?
I am bound for the promised land.

O'er all those wide extended plains
shines one eternal day;
there God the Son forever reigns,
and scatters night away. *Refrain*

No chilling winds or poisonous breath
can reach that healthful shore;
sickness and sorrow, pain and death,
are felt and feared no more. *Refrain*

When I shall reach that happy place,
I'll be forever blest,
for I shall see my Father's face,
and in his bosom rest. *Refrain*
—Word by Samuel Stennett

### Blest Be the Tie That Binds

Blest be the tie that binds
our hearts in Christian love;
the fellowship of kindred minds
is like to that above.

Before our Father's throne
we pour our ardent prayers;
our fears, our hopes, our aims are one,
our comforts and our cares.

We share each other's woes,
our mutual burdens bear;
and often for each other flows
the sympathizing tear.
When we asunder part,
it gives us inward pain;
but we shall still be joined in heart,
and hope to meet again.
—Words by John Fawcett

## God Be with You till We Meet Again

God be with you till we meet again;
by his counsels guide, uphold you,
with his sheep securely fold you;
God be with you till we meet again.
Till we meet, till we meet,
till we meet at Jesus' feet;
till we meet, till we meet,
God be with you till we meet again.
—Words by Jeremiah E. Rankin

## Nearer My God to Thee

Nearer, my God, to thee, nearer to thee!
E'en though it be a cross that raiseth me,
still all my song shall be, nearer, my God, to thee;
Nearer, my God, to thee, nearer to thee!

Though like the wanderer, the sun gone down,
darkness be over me, my rest a stone;
yet in my dreams I'd be nearer, my God, to thee;
Nearer, my God, to thee, nearer to thee!

Or if, on joyful wing cleaving the sky,
sun, moon, and stars forgot, upward I fly,
still all my song shall be, nearer, my God to thee;
Nearer, my God, to thee, nearer to thee!
—Words by Sarah F. Adams

## Savior, Like a Shepherd Lead Us

Savior, like a shepherd lead us,
much we need thy tender care;
in thy pleasant pastures feed us,
for our use thy folds prepare.

Blessed Jesus, blessed Jesus!
Thou has bought us, thine we are. *Repeat*

Early let us seek thy favor,
early let us do thy will;
blessed Lord and only Savior,
with thy love our bosoms fill.

Blessed Jesus, blessed Jesus!
Thou hast loved us, love us still. *Repeat*
—Words Attr. to Dorothy A. Thrupp

### He Leadeth Me

He leadeth me: O blessed thought!
O words with heavenly comfort fraught!
Whate'er I do, where'er I be,
still 'tis God's hand that leadeth me.

*Refrain*
He leadeth me, he leadeth me,
by his own hand he leadeth me;
his faithful follower I would be,
for by his hand he leadeth me.

And when my task on earth is done,
when by thy grace the victory's won,
e'en death's cold wave I will not flee,
since God through Jordan leadeth me. *Refrain*
—Words by Joseph H. Gilmore

# WITH CHILDREN

### Jesus Loves Me

Jesus loves me! This I know,
for the Bible tells me so.
Little ones to him belong;
they are weak, but he is strong.

*Refrain*
Yes, Jesus loves me! Yes, Jesus loves me!
Yes, Jesus loves me! The Bible tells me so.

Jesus loves me! This I know,
as he loved so long ago,
taking children on his knee,
saying, "Let them come to me." *Refrain*
—Words by St.1 Anna B. Wainer; St.2 David Rutherford McGuire

## This Is My Father's World

This is my Father's world, and to my listening ears
all nature sings, and round me rings
the music of the spheres.
This is my Father's world: I rest me in the thought
of rocks and trees, of skies and seas;
his hand the wonders wrought.
—Words by Maltbie D. Babcock

# IN ANY SITUATION

## Amazing Grace

Amazing grace! How sweet the sound
that saved a wretch like me!
I once was lost, but now am found;
was blind, but now I see.

'Twas grace that taught my heart to fear,
and grace my fears relieved;
how precious did that grace appear
the hour I first believed.

Through many dangers toils, and snares,
I have already come;
'tis grace hath brought me safe thus far,
and grace will lead me home.

Yea, when this flesh and heart shall fail,
and mortal life shall cease,
I shall possess, within the veil,
a life of joy and peace.

When we've been there ten thousand years,
bright shining as the sun,
we've no less days to sing God's praise
than when we'd first begun.
—Words by John Newton

### Praise God, from Whom All Blessings Flow (Doxology)
Praise God, from whom all blessings flow;
praise [God,] all creatures here below;
praise [God] above, ye heavenly host;
praise Father, Son, and Holy Ghost.
—Words by Thomas Ken

### A Mighty Fortress Is Our God
A mighty fortress is our God,
a bulwark never failing;
our helper he amid the flood
of mortal ills prevailing.
For still our ancient foe doth seek to work us woe;
his craft and power are great,
and armed with cruel hate,
on earth is not his equal.

Did we in our own strength confide,
our striving would be losing,
were not the right man on our side,
the man of God's own choosing.
Dost ask who that may be? Christ Jesus, it is he;
Lord Sabaoth, his name, from age to age the same,
and he must win the battle.
—Words by Martin Luther

## Jesus Keep Me Near the Cross

Jesus, keep me near the cross;
there a precious fountain,
free to all, a healing stream,
flows from Calvary's mountain.

*Refrain*
In the cross, in the cross, be my glory ever,
till my raptured soul shall find rest beyond the river.

Near the cross I'll watch and wait,
hoping, trusting ever,
till I reach the golden strand
just beyond the river. *Refrain*
—Words by Fanny J. Crosby

## What a Friend We Have in Jesus

What a friend we have in Jesus,
all our sins and griefs to bear!
What a privilege to carry
everything to God in prayer!
O what peace we often forfeit,
O what needless pain we bear,
all because we do not carry
everything to God in prayer.

Are we weak and heavy laden,
cumbered with a load of care?
Precious Savior, still our refuge;
take it to the Lord in prayer.
Do thy friends despise, forsake thee?
Take it to the Lord in prayer!
In his arms he'll take and shield thee;
thou wilt find a solace there.
—Words by Joseph M. Scriven

# CHAPTER FOUR

# TRADITIONAL BLESSINGS, PRAYERS, AND SCRIPTURE SUGGESTIONS

## TRADITIONAL BLESSINGS

### Traditional Gaelic Blessing
May the road rise to meet you.
May the wind be always at your back.
May the sun shine warm upon your face.
May the rains fall softly upon your fields
and until we meet again
may God hold you in the palm of his hand. Amen.

### God Be in Your Head
God be in your head, and in your understanding.
God be in your eyes, and in your looking.
God be in your mouth, and in your speaking.
God be in your heart, and in your thinking.
God be in your end, and at your departing.
—Old Sarum Blessing

# TRADITIONAL PRAYERS

### Prayer of Saint Thomas Aquinas

Give us, O Lord, steadfast hearts,
which no unworthy thought can drag downward,
unconquered hearts, which no tribulation can wear out,
upright hearts, which no unworthy purpose may tempt aside.
Bestow upon us also, O Lord our God,
understanding to know you, diligence to seek you,
wisdom to find you,
and a faithfulness that may finally embrace you;
through Jesus Christ our Lord. Amen.
—Saint Thomas Aquinas, 13th century

### The Prayer of Saint Francis of Assisi

Lord, make me an instrument of thy peace;
where there is hatred, let me sow love;
where there is injury, pardon;
where there is doubt, faith;
where there is despair, hope;
where there is darkness, light;
and where there is sadness, joy.

O Divine Master,
grant that I may not so much seek
to be consoled as to console;
to be understood, as to understand;
to be loved, as to love.
For it is in giving that we receive,
it is in pardoning that we are pardoned,
and it is in dying that we are born to eternal life.
—Francis of Assisi

### The Lord's Prayer, Traditional

Our Father, who art in heaven, hallowed be thy name.
Thy kingdom come,
thy will be done on earth as it is in heaven.

Give us this day our daily bread.
And forgive us our trespasses,
as we forgive those who trespass against us.
And lead us not into temptation,
but deliver us from evil.
For thine is the kingdom, and the power, and the glory, forever.
Amen.

### The Lord's Prayer, Ecumenical

Our Father in heaven,
hallowed be your name,
your kingdom come,
your will be done, on earth as in heaven.
Give us today our daily bread.
Forgive us our sins
as we forgive those who sin against us.
Save us from the time of trial
and deliver us from evil.
For the kingdom, the power, and the glory are yours
now and for ever. Amen.

# BENEDICTIONS FROM SCRIPTURE

### Numbers 6:24-26

The LORD bless you and keep you;
The LORD make his face to shine upon you,
    and be gracious to you;
The LORD lift up his countenance upon you,
    and give you peace.

### Romans 15:13

May the God of hope fill you with all joy and peace in believing,
so that you may abound in hope by the power of the Holy Spirit.

**Romans 16:25-27**
Now to God who is able to strengthen you according to my gospel and the proclamation of Jesus Christ, according to the revelation of the mystery that was kept secret for long ages but is now disclosed, and through the prophetic writings is made known to all the Gentiles, according to the command of the eternal God, to bring about the obedience of faith—to the only wise God, through Jesus Christ, to whom be the glory forever! Amen.

# ADDITIONAL SCRIPTURE SUGGESTIONS

*See the Scripture Index for page references to the passages listed throughout the book. The following are two additional passages, often requested by patients.*

### Psalm 23 (KJV)
The LORD is my shepherd; I shall not want.
He maketh me to lie down in green pastures:
    he leadeth me beside the still waters;
He restoreth my soul: he leadeth me in the
    paths of righteousness for his name's sake.
Yea, though I walk through the valley of the shadow of death,
    I will fear no evil: for thou art with me; thy rod and
    thy staff, they comfort me.
Thou preparest a table before me in the presence
    of mine enemies: thou anoinest my head with oil,
    my cup runneth over.
Surely goodness and mercy shall follow me all the days of my
    life: and I will dwell in the house of the LORD for ever.

### Psalm 100
Make a joyful noise to the LORD, all the earth.
Worship the LORD, with gladness; come into his presence with
    singing.

Know that the LORD is God. It is he that made us,
    and we are his; we are his people,
    and the sheep of his pasture.
Enter his gates with thanksgiving and his courts with praise.
    Give thanks to him, bless his name.
For the LORD,is good; his steadfast love endures forever,
    and his faithfulness to all generations.

# CHAPTER FIVE

# GUIDED PRAYERS

When patients are strongly connected to the worshiping community and comfortable with personal prayer, use the *bidding prayer* format to help engage them in creating their own prayers for healing. Form *pastoral prayers* in response to the patient's answers to a series of questions. *Breath prayers* are simple phrase prayers that speak of the patient's most critical need.

## BIDDING PRAYER

Bidding prayers are a classic form of prayer where a leader invites, or bids, persons to pray for particular needs in a guided way, with the response either spoken or unspoken. A time of request and answer are followed by a collect that addresses the need. In more personal prayer, there may be only one collect at the end of the prayer. The Lord's Prayer may also end the time of prayer.

### Example of a Bidding Prayer

Let us pray for all the people of our church (*Silence for prayer*).

**Collect:** O God, you nourish and sustain us by your Word and Sacrament. Strengthen the people of our church, especially Betty and the women of her circle group as they minister to her in the hospital. May the service and witness of our congregation be faithful to your desires. We pray in Jesus' name. **Amen.**

Let us pray for all who suffer illness, distress, or grief *(Silence for prayer)*. Compassionate God, you are a wellspring of comfort and healing. Grant comfort, rest, and release to those in need, especially our sister Betty as she recovers. We pray in Jesus' name. **Amen.**

Let us pray for whatever else we need *(Silence for prayer)*. God of Love, hear the prayers of your people. Enliven us, by your Spirit, to live into the fullness of your reign. We pray through Jesus, our life and our hope. **Amen.**

# PASTORAL PRAYER

If patients are able, have them respond to the following questions, then weave their answer together in a prayer.

- What is the term you use most often for God?
- What do you need to ask God for the most?
- Who are you most concerned about during your illness?
- What would you like to ask for on their behalf?
- What are you most grateful for during this time?

## Example of a Pastoral Prayer Based on Patient's Responses

Eternal Lord, you know that Nora needs relief from the pain she is experiencing after surgery. We thank you she has come through her knee replacement so well, and will soon be walking well again. We remember her children, and pray you would help them not worry too much or fuss over her in unsupportive ways when she returns home. We thank you for your healing presence, made real to her through her Sunday school class. We pray in Jesus' name. Amen.

# BREATH PRAYER

Many persons have been aided by the use of a breath prayer. This form simplifies prayer into a mantra that patients can pray at various times, using their breathing to offer the prayer and maintain focus. It often becomes a phrase that helps a patient through a difficult procedure, or while they await pain medication. I also convey that I will use their breath prayer for myself, and will remember them when I do so.

This form of prayer provides intimate sharing between patient and pastor, and can be shared over the phone when a return visit is not possible. The basic form of a breath prayer is calling God by name as you inhale, and offering the greatest need as you exhale. The words do not have to be spoken aloud. If patients are able, have them respond to the following questions, then choose, or form, a breath prayer from their responses:

- What is your favorite way to address God?
- What is it you feel you need the most at this time?

## Examples of Breath Prayers

- Loving God, give me peace.
- Holy Spirit, give me strength.
- Jesus, let me be strong.

# CHAPTER SIX

# RITUALS

## ACCEPTING CHRIST

Some patients we encounter have not been part of the life of the church, and have not established a commitment to honor and serve God. Often, illness brings them to a new understanding of the meaning of life, and they are ready to reach out to God. Here is a simple ritual to use in helping a patient make a commitment to trust in Jesus.

### Ritual for Accepting Christ

**Preparation**
*Have a small vial of anointing oil available. Some token of faith reminder, such as a pocket cross or prayer card, would be appropriate to leave with the patient as a reminder of the commitment made.*

**Invitation**
While Jesus was here on earth, he called people to be his disciples and follow him; today, by God's Spirit, he still calls us to follow and trust in him. You have voiced your willingness to move closer to God.

### Prayer

Dearest God, I know you are calling Eduardo to follow, to put his trust in you, and I praise your holy name for loving him so much, and inviting him to walk in your ways and come to know you more deeply. Guide him into closeness with you so that whatever comes of this illness, he will know that your love and grace are with him, in Jesus' name. Amen.

Eduardo, I invite you to pray with me by repeating after me:
Dearest God,
I want to respond to your call.
I want to follow Jesus.
I want to allow the Holy Spirit to fill my life.
I know there are things in my life that get in the way;
    please take away everything that separates me from you.
I want to believe in you, even though I don't always know
    how to do that.
Change and transform me in the ways you want to.
Help me give all of my life and all of my being over to you.
Grant healing and wholeness to my spirit.
And, if it is your will, heal this body,
    so that in renewed life and vitality,
I may serve you with all my heart, my soul, my mind,
    and my body. Amen.

*Follow with anointing with oil by making the sign of the cross on the person's forehead.*


# BAPTISM

There are times when a patient who has not been a part of a church fellowship expresses desire to be baptized. Illness may have led to a reconsideration of spiritual life, and they feel immediacy about being baptized. The baptismal covenant, however, is best expressed within a covenant community during a public service of worship. If the patient is not in a medical crisis, and there are family members who are part of a specific tradition apart from your own, it may be appropriate to talk with the patient about involving the family pastor and waiting until a catechetical process is completed.

There are times, however, when baptism is requested and should be performed in the hospital setting, as in the case of a child facing imminent death. It should be stressed that, while many traditions see baptism as an appropriate rite of initiation into the family of Christ, many do not teach denial of full salvation to infants who die before they are baptized. United Methodism, in particular, "has always strongly affirmed the biblical teaching that Christ died for all, and that God's prevenient grace is available to all and is sufficient for such children" (*The United Methodist Book of Worship*, p. 83). The following ritual is adapted from *The United Methodist Book of Worship* (Baptismal Covenant II-A, pp. 95, 100-102). It is used by permission.

# Ritual for Baptism

### Preparation
*Before beginning, secure a small bowl of water.*

### Invitation
[My brother/sister] in Christ:
Through the sacrament of baptism
    we are initiated into Christ's holy Church.
We are incorporated into God's mighty acts of salvation
    and given new birth through water and the Spirit.
All of this is God's gift, offered to us without price.

### Renunciation of Sin and Profession of Faith
*Address these questions directly to the person being baptized or to the parents of children unable to respond for themselves.*
    On behalf of the whole Church, I ask you:
    Do you reject all that is evil, repent of your sin,
    and accept the freedom and power God gives you
        to resist evil, injustice, and oppression
        in whatever forms they present themselves?
    **I do.**

Do you confess Jesus Christ as your Savior,
put your whole trust in his grace,
and promise to serve him as your Lord,
in union with the Church which Christ has opened
    to people of all ages, nations, and races?
**I do.**

### Prayer Over the Water

Eternal Father, your mighty acts of salvation
    have been made known through water—
from the moving of your Spirit upon the waters of creation,
to the deliverance of your people
    through the flood and through the Red Sea.
In the fullness of time you sent Jesus,
    nurtured in the water of a womb,
    baptized by John, and anointed by your Spirit.
He called his disciples
    to share in the baptism of his death and resurrection and to
        make disciples of all nations.
Pour out your Holy Spirit,
    to bless this gift of water and *this one/those* who *receives/*
      *receive* it,
    to wash away *her/his/their* sin and clothe *her/his/them* in
      righteousness throughout *her/his/their life/lives*
that, dying and being raised with Christ,
    *he/she/they* may share in his final victory;
through the same Jesus Christ our Lord. Amen.

### Act of Baptism

*Place water on the head three times*
    *Name*, I baptize you in the name of the Father,
    and of the Son, and of the Holy Spirit. Amen.

### Anointing

*Anoint with oil by making a sign of the cross on the forehead.*
    *Name*, The Holy Spirit work within you,
    that being born through water and the Spirit,
    you may be a faithful disciple of Jesus Christ

and know the hope of Christ's eternal kingdom. Amen.
The God of all grace, who has called us
to eternal glory in Christ,
and sustains us by the power of the Holy Spirit,
bless, preserve, and keep you, now and forever. Amen.

# HOLY COMMUNION

Many Christian traditions have provisions for taking communion to those who are unable to attend the service of Holy Communion in their local congregation, as a means of extending the table in fellowship to all. Since the bread and wine will have already been consecrated in the worship service, either clergy or laity may conduct this brief order.

When giving Communion in a hospital room, care should be taken to preserve an attitude of reverence, even though this service may feel a little awkward due the surroundings.

## Ritual for Holy Communion

### Preparation
*The bread and wine should be put on a flat surface within easy reach of the minister. An invitation to partake of the elements should be extended to any baptized Christians who are present in the room.*

*Depending on the circumstances, the Communion minister may begin with a scripture reading (possibly from the lectionary), a hymn that might be sung from memory (a stanza of "Amazing Grace," for example), and an intercessory prayer (perhaps taken from this book).*

### Prayer
Loving God, who knows our every need: By the power of your Holy Spirit, bless those who receive this sacrament of the body and blood of Jesus Christ your Son. Strengthen them for the challenge of this day and heal them for the work of tomorrow. For you are our life and health, our strength in every trouble, our

hope in every struggle. As those who share in the body of Christ, teach us to pray boldly the prayer he taught us: Our Father who art in heaven ...

## Serving the Elements
*Give the elements with these or other appropriate words:*
  Name, The Body of Christ given for you.
  Name, The Blood of the New Covenant poured out
        for our salvation.
*If the person is not able to consume the bread or wine due to illness, it is perfectly acceptable to place a very small particle in the mouth or to touch the bread to the lips. If this is not possible, it may be helpful to explain that the Christian Church has always taught that the desire to receive Communion in such circumstances is itself the true Communion in Jesus Christ.*

## Closing
*The minister may then say or sing a doxology, such as:*
  Praise God from whom all blessings flow ...

# ANOINTING WITH OIL FOR HEALING

The purpose of anointing is to connect the patient with the healing power of Christ's death and resurrection. Anointing is an action to bring healing, not only to physical needs, but to relationships, emotions, and memories as well. The following liturgy is adapted from *The United Methodist Book of Worship*, pp. 615, 620-21. It is used by permission.

## Ritual for Anointing with Oil

### Preparation
*Have a small vial of olive oil available. Invite others who are present in the room to participate by receiving anointing as well.*

### Invitation
  We have come to lift up our brothers and sisters before the
    Lord, that they might receive healing.

## Prayer

Almighty and everlasting God,
who can banish all affliction both of soul and body,
show forth your power upon those in need,
that by your mercy they may be restored to serve you afresh
in holiness of living, through Jesus Christ our Lord. Amen.

## Pastoral Prayer Over the Oil

O God, the giver of health and salvation,
    we give thanks to you for the gift of oil.
As your holy apostles anointed many who were sick
        and healed them,
    so pour out your Holy Spirit on us and on this gift,
    that those who in faith and repentance receive this
        anointing may be made whole;
    through Jesus Christ our Lord. Amen.

## Anointing

*Make the sign of the cross on the forehead and say:*
    *Name(s),* Receive this blessing in the name of the Father, Son
        and Holy Spirit. Amen.

## Closing Prayer

Almighty God, we pray that *(our brothers and sisters)* may be
        comforted in *their* suffering and made whole.
When they are afraid, give them courage;
when they feel weak, grant them your strength;
when they are afflicted, afford them patience;
when they are lost, offer them hope;
when they are alone, move *(the community/caregivers/*
        *particular persons)* to their side;
*(if appropriate)* when death comes, open your arms to receive
        *(Name).*

In the name of Jesus Christ we pray. Amen.

As Jesus taught us, we are bold to pray together:
    Our Father, who art in heaven...

# SCRIPTURE INDEX